# PATIENT, DOCTOR SOCIETY

*A symposium of introspections*

# PATIENT

# DOCTOR

# SOCIETY

**A symposium of introspections**

CONTRIBUTORS

FERGUSON ANDERSON, PAUL BEESON, ROY CALNE
CEDRIC CARTER, HARRY HARRIS, GEORGE KNOX, ALBERT KUSHLICK
MICHAEL LAURENCE, HENRY MILLER, LIONEL PENROSE
GEORGE PICKERING, MARTIN ROTH, PETER SCOTT
GEOFFREY SPENCER

Edited by Gordon McLachlan

Published for the
Nuffield Provincial Hospitals Trust
by the Oxford University Press
London New York Toronto
1972

*Oxford University Press Ely House, London, W1*
GLASGOW NEW YORK TORONTO MELBOURNE WELLINGTON
CAPE TOWN SALISBURY IBADAN NAIROBI DAR ES SALAAM LUSAKA ADDIS ABABA
BOMBAY CALCUTTA MADRAS KARACHI LAHORE DACCA
KUALA LUMPUR SINGAPORE HONG KONG TOKYO

ISBN 0 19 721367 7



*Designed by Bernard Crossland*

PRINTED IN GREAT BRITAIN
BY BURGESS AND SON (ABINGDON) LTD
ABINGDON, BERKS

# CONTENTS

# FOREWORD

## BY HENRY MILLER

THE symposium recorded in this volume had its origin in a short paper entitled 'Real goals for medicine', published in *Science Journal* in October 1969. This discussed some unsolved problems of priority, evaluation, and ethics raised by the scientific revolution in medicine. The dependence of informed decisions in these difficult fields on a continuing dialogue between public and profession was stressed, and the possibility of a series of medical 'Pugwash' conferences was mentioned as a potentially useful instrument of such discussions. The suggestion attracted the interest of the Department of Health, and the Nuffield Provincial Hospitals Trust which sponsored and arranged the first forum of which this is an account.

The difficulties that presently evoke so unfamiliar a mood of introspection in the medical profession are numerous, and the choice of subject for the first conference had to be made from an embarrassment of riches. The problems of an ageing population? 'Big' versus 'little' medicine? An attempt to agree a list of major priorities? A study of cost-effectiveness—but it is so easy to invent a figure for cost and so difficult to measure effectiveness? Finally we decided to restrict our first effort to the analysis of a discrete but manageable and highly sensitive area of the general problem that has been created by the conspicuous success of modern medicine in preventing and controlling many serious diseases and in maintaining life in previously fatal illness. The symposium reported here concerns a series of situations in which it can be argued that the interests of the individual patient and those of the society of which he is a member are in conflict—situations where the physician's traditional devotion to the individual patient might from one point of view even be regarded as antisocial.

The subjects discussed emphasize the preoccupations of those concerned in making the selection. They include the long-term eugenic problems inseparable from the survival to reproductive age of treated subjects of hereditary diseases; the care of children and adults with profound mental subnormality; the quality of survival in infants treated surgically for grave congenital deformities; the value and socio-economic implications of intensive therapy, renal dialysis, and transplantation; the care of the aged; the intractable social problems posed by aggressive psychopathy; and finally a wise and judicial essay by Dr Paul Beeson on the quality of survival.

All these and other marginal issues are discussed in the following pages. The reader will look in vain for easy or ready-made solutions to any of the problems, but if the papers and briefly abstracted discussions leave most questions unanswered, there are few that have not been raised.

In most respects the record of the symposium remains up-to-date. Many clinicians are still concerned at what they regard as the complacency of the geneticist in the face of our deliberate augmentation of the pool of unfavourable genes. The great difficulty of recruiting an adequate number of suitable staff to furnish acceptable care for the mentally subnormal remains, and lends force to the demand for an intensive and adequately funded research programme into the cause and prevention of intellectual retardation, which represents the best hope of coping with this tragic situation in the long term. With regard to intensive care, we jib at its expense—but would like it for our families. Most physicians feel that the haemodyalisis–transplantation routine is now so well established as a life-saving device that we should make even greater efforts to extend its availability to young sufferers from chronic kidney disease. The problems of the aged remain unsolved: retirement at 65 may be hard on the elderly, but later retirement would often be hard on the rest of us. So far as psychopathy is concerned the need is surely for a new type of institution with some features of a prison and some of a hospital—and with an attempted rehabilitation of indeterminate duration.

There is only one aspect in which a significant development has occurred during the interval between the symposium and publication, and this concerns the management of spina bifida. The results of surgical treatment of no less than 1,200 unselected cases of myelomeningocele in Sheffield were reported to a recent meeting of the British Paediatric Association. The results were the best yet recorded, but they were profoundly disappointing. In general they support the epidemiologist's prediction that reasonable results can be expected only in milder cases, and that indiscriminate surgery imposes prolonged suffering on the individual as well as an unbearable load on the family and society.

When the more dramatic and esoteric advances in medicine are set aside its major problems loom large—the care of the handicapped and the aged. Often this can find no possible justification in social efficiency or cost-effectiveness. In the last resort even the materialist must admit that the justification for medicine is a moral one.

*Newcastle upon Tyne*
*July 1971*

# LIST OF PARTICIPANTS

*Joint Chairmen*

Sir GEORGE PICKERING, D Sc, MA, MD, FRCP, FRS. *Master of Pembroke College, Oxford, and Chairman of the Trust's Medical Consultative Committee*

Dr HENRY MILLER, MD, FRCP. *Vice-Chancellor, University of Newcastle upon Tyne*

---

Professor PAUL B. BEESON, MD, FRCP. *Nuffield Professor of Clinical Medicine, University of Oxford*

Dr J. H. F. BROTHERSTON, MA, MD, FRCP, FRSE, DPH. *Chief Medical Officer, Scottish Home and Health Department*

Professor R. Y. CALNE, MA, MS, FRCS. *Professor of Surgery, University of Cambridge*

Dr C. O. CARTER, DM, FRCP. *Director, Medical Research Council Genetics Unit*

Professor C. T. DOLLERY, FRCP. *Professor of Clinical Pharmacology, Royal Postgraduate Medical School*

Professor W. FERGUSON ANDERSON, OBE, MD, FRCP. *Professor of Geriatric Medicine, University of Glasgow*

Sir GEORGE GODBER, GCB, DM, FRCP, DPH. *Chief Medical Officer, Department of Health and Social Security*

Professor HARRY HARRIS, MD, MRCP, FRS. *Galton Professor of Human Genetics, University College London*

Professor D. N. S. KERR, FRCP. *Professor of Medicine, University of Newcastle upon Tyne*

Professor E. G. KNOX, MD, MRCP. *Professor of Social Medicine, University of Birmingham*

Dr A. KUSHLICK, MRCP, DPH. *Director of Research into Subnormality, Wessex Regional Hospital Board*

Dr K. M. LAURENCE, MA, MB, FRCPath. *Senior Lecturer in Paediatric Pathology, Welsh National School of Medicine*

Professor T. McKEOWN, PhD, DPhil, MD, FRCP. *Professor of Social Medicine, University of Birmingham*

Mr GORDON McLACHLAN, CBE. *Secretary, Nuffield Provincial Hospitals Trust*

Dr S. G. OWEN, MD, FRCP. *Second Secretary, Medical Research Council*

Professor L. S. PENROSE, MA, MD, DSc, FRCP, FRS. *Research Director, Kennedy-Galton Centre for Mental Retardation Research and Diagnosis*

Mr TIMOTHY RAISON, MP

Professor MARTIN ROTH, MD, FRCP, FRCPsych. *Professor of Psychological Medicine, University of Newcastle upon Tyne and Member of the Trust's Medical Consultative Committee*

Dr P. D. SCOTT, MA, MD, FRCP, FRCPsych. *Consultant Physician, The Maudsley Hospital*

Dr G. T. SPENCER, FFA, RCS. *Consultant in charge of the Intensive Therapy Unit, St Thomas's Hospital*

Sir GEORGE WALLER, QC.

Miss KATHERINE WHITEHORN. *Columnist, The Observer*

Dr HENRY YELLOWLEES, CB, FRCP. *Deputy Chief Medical Officer, Department of Health and Social Security*

# ACKNOWLEDGEMENTS

THANKS are especially due, not only to those who contributed papers to this symposium, but also to all those who participated in it and made it a memorable experience. Also to Miss Ellinor Grant who made such excellent précis of the discussions. Acknowledgement is also made to Blackwell Scientific Publications Ltd for permission to reproduce as Professor Calne's contribution (8), his introduction and chapter on 'Ethics, the Law and the Future' from *Clinical Organ Transplantation* (Blackwell, 1971).

G. McL.

# 1

# The treatment of genetically determined disorders and the effect of current policies on population eugenics


C. O. CARTER
DM, FRCP
*Director*
*Medical Research Council Genetics Unit*

# The treatment of genetically determined disorders and the effect of current policies on population eugenics

## Introduction

THERE is a real dilemma posed by the successful treatment of genetically and part genetically determined disease such that the patient's 'biological fitness' (that is his relative reproductive fitness) is raised. In theory, unless countermeasures are taken by genetic counselling or other means, the ultimate effect of such new treatments is to reduce the case mortality, but to allow a corresponding rise in the frequency of the condition until the total mortality is back to the original level. This dilemma will be discussed in relation to the three categories of genetically and part genetically determined disease:

(1) That due to chromosomal anomalies.

(2) That due to mutant genes of large effect.

(3) That due to a multifactorial aetiology—a combination of genetic predisposition based on genetic variation at several gene loci and environmental triggers.

## Chromosome disorders

The load of chromosomal anomalies is heavy at conception. As many as 6 per cent of conceptions may have a major chromosomal anomaly. Most of this, however, is dealt with by spontaneous abortion, and as much as 50 per cent of spontaneous first trimester abortions may be associated with a chromosome anomaly. Triploidy (69 chromosomes instead of the normal 46), trisomy of chromosome 16, and the XO genotype may each have a frequency at conception of nearly 1 per cent, but almost all foetuses with the first two conditions and about 98 per cent of those with the third terminate as first trimester abortions. The remainder of the XOs present as Turner's syndrome, with a low birth frequency of about 2 in 10,000. The autosomal trisomy which is most common at birth, that of a G chromosome, has a birth frequency of about 1 in 600, and this may represent an intra-uterine survival of about 40 per cent. The survivors have Down's syndrome (mongolism). Only the sex-chromosome trisomies—the triple X female, the XXY male (Klinefelter's syndrome), and the XYY male—appear to have no extra risk of abortion and each have a birth frequency of the order of 1 in 1,000 of the appropriate sex.

Any treatments which reduced the frequency with which foetuses with chromosome anomalies spontaneously abort would have serious public health implications; but there is no indication that any of the treatments for threatened miscarriage prevent spontaneous abortions which are due to chromosome anomalies. Further there are no treatments in prospect which would alter the reproductive fitness of those affected by chromosome anomalies. By its nature the anomalies involve many genes and the consequent abnormalities in the patient's biochemistry will be multiple and not easily corrected. In the case of mongolism it is known that where women patients do have children the proportion of these children affected is high, perhaps as much as 1 in 3.

If and when some treatment of mongolism were devised that would raise the fitness of mongols from near zero to near unity, unless countermeasures were taken, the rise in the birth frequency would be by 30 per cent per generation (or 15 per cent if the male patients tended to have normal children) that is more than doubling every hundred years. The situation would probably be the same with the other trisomies which may survive to the end of pregnancy, Edward's syndrome (17 trisomy), and Patau's syndrome (13 trisomy), if these were successfully treated. In the case of the sex chromosome anomalies the triple X women and XYY men both fortunately seem to produce mostly normal germ cells and have normal children. The XXY individuals (Klinefelter's syndrome) and the XOs are usually sterile. If any treatment was found which restored their biological fitness it would be necessary to see what sort of germ cells they produce, but it is perhaps likely that they too would mostly have normal children.

## Conditions due to mutant genes of large effect

The prospect of effective treatment for these conditions is relatively good, since there is likely to be one specific biochemical abnormality. Some effective treatments are already available: dietary avoidance therapy for phenylketonuria and galactosaemia; palliative drug therapy for Kinnier-Wilson's disease; surgery for multiple polyposis of the colon and hereditary spherocytosis. The rate of rise in the birth frequency of such disorders will be much influenced by the precise mode of inheritance: rapid for dominant conditions, slow for recessive conditions, and intermediate for X-linked conditions.

### DOMINANT CONDITIONS

The birth frequency for dominant conditions where patients are heterozygous for the mutant gene involved depends directly on the mutation rate of the gene, and the biological fitness of the patients. When fitness is zero the birth frequency is simply twice the mutation rate. Each mutant gene affects one patient, who does not reproduce. Gene mutations are rare events and so the birth frequency of such conditions will be low. A new treatment which raises the fitness of patients to 0·5 will, with no countermeasures, lead to a rise in birth frequency until the establishment of a new equilibrium when the birth frequency is doubled, that is at four times the mutation rate. Each mutant gene will then on average persist two generations and affect two individuals.

The rise in birth frequency is rapid, half of it occurring in one generation and three-quarters in two generations and seven-eighths in three generations. With a more successful treatment, which raises fitness to 0·9, the birth frequency rises till a new equilibrium is reached at ten times the original birth frequency, that is twenty times the mutation rate. The initial rise would be rapid, the birth frequency nearly doubling after one generation and increasing more than fourfold after four generations and more than half the ultimate rise is achieved in six generations. With a mutation rate of 1 in 100,000 and an initial birth frequency of 1 in 50,000 a ten-fold rise, due to a rise in fitness to 0·9, would still leave the birth frequency at only 1 in 5,000. However, a similar rise for the several hundred dominant conditions known would be serious. With a fully effective treatment, such that fitness became 1·0, the rise in birth frequency would be simply an addition of the original frequency in each generation, so that this frequency would be twice the initial frequency after one generation, three times after two generations, and so on. But as the gene frequency rose homozygotes would start appearing and if, as is likely, these were severe and lethal (for example patients who are homozygotes for the gene for achondroplasia die perinatally) this would limit the rise at a birth frequency of affected heterozygotes of about 1 in 300.

RECESSIVE CONDITIONS

The principles governing the relationship between the birth frequency of a condition and the fitness of patients is similar to that for dominants, but changes are very much slower. In the equilibrium state, and where the heterozygous carrier has a fitness of 1·0, the birth frequency of lethal recessive conditions is the same as the mutation rate. Patients are homozygous for the mutant gene and two mutant genes are lost whenever a patient dies without reproducing. In contrast to dominants the relationship between the occurrence of the mutation and the birth of an affected child may be remote. For a typically rare recessive lethal condition with a birth frequency of say 1 in 90,000, the mean interval, without inbreeding, between the occurrence of the mutation and its meeting with another gene of the same kind in a patient is some 300 generations, that is about 8,000 years. Further for every mutant gene in a patient there are 299 in heterozygous carriers. The effect of raising the fitness of patients from zero to, say, 0·9 will be to raise the total number of mutant genes in the population, and so the birth frequency of patients in successive generations by only a small fraction. After one generation the rise in the birth frequency of the condition will only be 0·3 per cent and the rise in the gene frequency will also be only 0·3 per cent. It will be many hundreds of generations before the full tenfold increase in birth frequency is reached and it would take some 150 generations, over 4,000 years, for the birth frequency to double.

Just a few recessive conditions are relatively common in local populations. Cystic fibrosis probably has a frequency of a little more than 1 in 2,000, say 1 in 1,600, in most European populations, implying a gene frequency of about 1 in 40. If this high frequency had been maintained by a correspondingly high mutation rate then the effect of raising fitness to 0·9 would be a 4·5 per cent rise in frequency per generation and this would be fairly rapid. There is, however, good reason to suppose that such high frequencies depend, not on an unusually high mutation rate, but on heterozygote advantage, that is that the relatively common heterozygotes actually have some selective advantage. In this situation, changes in birth frequency will be much more rapidly influenced by any medical advances which alter the degree of heterozygote advantage than by those which affect the fitness of patients. The frequency of the sickle-cell gene is lower in American Negroes (after allowance is made for white admixture) than in West Africans because the heterozygote advantage against malaria is lost in America, even though the mortality of the homozygous patients is less in America than in West Africa. Even if the fitness of patients were raised to unity and at the same time the heterozygote advantage was lost, the gene frequency would only very slowly rise. On the other hand, if the heterozygote advantage persists and the fitness of patients is substantially raised there will be a fairly rapid rise (depending on the degree of heterozygote advantage) in the birth frequency of patients. The ultimate equilibrium will depend, not on the degree of heterozygote advantage, but on the relative reproductive fitness of the two homozygotes.

### X-LINKED RECESSIVE CONDITIONS

With X-linked recessive conditions due to mutant genes on the X-chromosome the effect of successful new treatment on the birth frequency is intermediate between the rapid rise expected with dominants and the very slow rise expected with recessive conditions. Where fitness is zero the birth frequency in males at equilibrium is three times the mutation rate, 1 in 30,000 where, say, the mutation rate is again, say, 1 in 90,000. This is made up of 1 in 90,000 males affected by fresh mutation and 1 in 45,000 born to heterozygous carrier women. Once again the effect of raising fitness from zero to, say, 0·9 will ultimately, without countermeasures, be to raise the frequency of affected males from 1 in 30,000 to 1 in 3,000. For the first generation after the new treatment there is no increase in affected males since those enabled to reproduce by the new treatment will have normal sons but carrier daughters. The increase in carrier women will, however, be reflected in the males of the second generation among whom the increase in birth frequency will be about 12 per cent, the doubling time would be about five generations, and half the ultimate rise would be achieved in some fifteen generations.

As the gene frequency rose homozygous affected girls would start to appear. These girl patients would probably be no more severely affected than the male patients and so the treatment would probably be as effective with them as with the male patients. This would, however, only slightly affect the equilibrium birth frequency in males since when the birth frequency of affected males is, say, 1 in 3,000, that of affected girls will only be 1 in 9,000,000.

## Conditions with multifactorial aetiology

No simple calculations may yet be made of the effects of new treatments on the birth frequency of conditions where the aetiology depends on more complex mechanisms of inheritance. The presence of a substantial environmental component in the aetiology of most of these conditions makes it possible for the frequency of these conditions to be greatly altered, at least for some time, by purely environmental changes.

The nature of the genetic predisposition to common malformations such as neural tube malformations, anencephaly, and spina bifida, which are now the commonest cause of still-birth in Britain, or the congenital heart malformations which are the commonest specific cause of infant death, or pyloric stenosis the commonest condition requiring abdominal surgery in infancy, is very probably an accumulation of genes none in themselves abnormal, but acting in the same direction to give marked deviation from the population mean. The process is similar to the genetic determination of tall stature, or of most high blood pressure, or, at the other end of the scale, of the milder degrees of mental subnormality. Individuals who genetically are marked deviants from the population mean are at risk of developing the malformation if additional environmental triggers also come into play. It is possible to represent this diagrammatically with genetic predisposition on the $x$ axis, inserting a threshold beyond which individuals are at risk, as in Figure 1.1. Alternatively one may put the total 'liability' along the $x$ axis, this liability including both genetic predisposition and any environmental predisposing

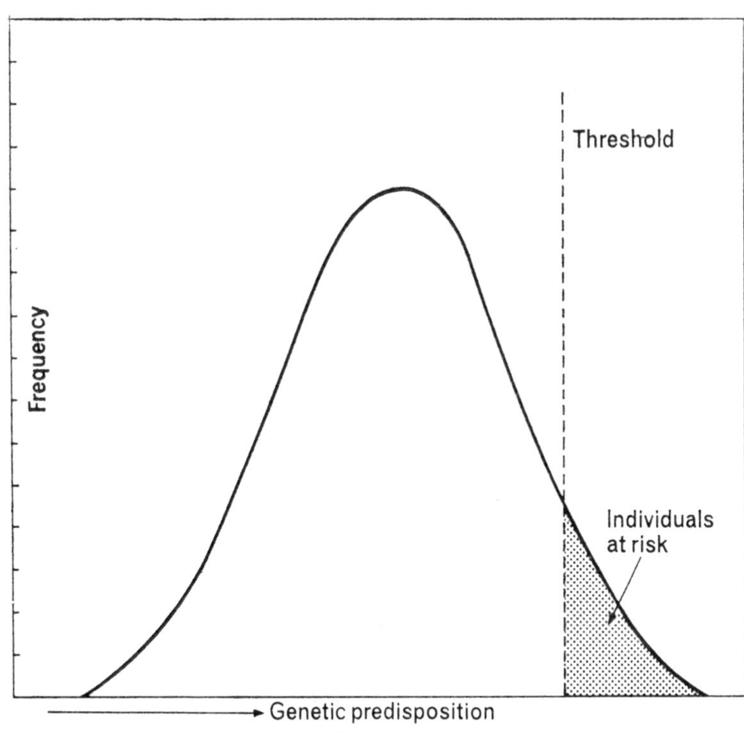


**Figure 1.1**

factors, and then *all* individuals beyond the threshold are affected, as in Figure 1.2.

Models of this kind explain very well the family patterns, that is, the proportion of monozygotic and dizygotic co-twins of index patients also affected and of sibs, offspring, and second- and third-degree relatives also affected, given by the congenital malformations. The second type of model also makes possible a rough estimate of the heritability of the condition, that is the proportion of the variance in the total liability in the population that is due to genetic variation. It is this 'heritability' which determines the genetic response of the population to any change in the selection against affected individuals. In most common malformations the estimates of heritability are fairly high, of the order of 60–80 per cent.

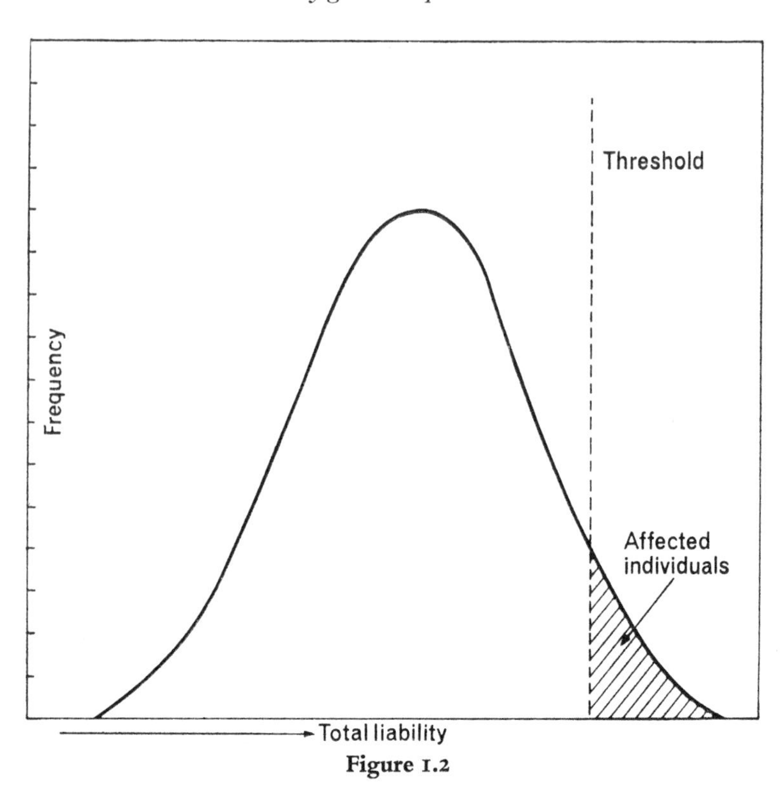


**Figure 1.2**

The same kind of aetiology probably applies to many common disorders of adult life, such as duodenal ulcer or schizophrenia, or diabetes mellitus, or even rheumatoid arthritis.

It is, however, difficult to explain the high frequency of some of these conditions when they markedly reduce reproductive fitness. The neural tube malformations have a birth frequency in Britain of about 1 in 200, the heart malformations together of about 1 in 160, schizophrenia of about 1 in 100. It is possible that some of these frequencies do not represent an equilibrium, but are temporarily raised as a result of environmental changes. This is certainly the case, for example, with ischaemic heart disease. The neural tube malformations show variations in birth frequency within Britain which are difficult to explain solely in genetic terms and so these malformations may be out of equilibrium.

There is no indication of such disequilibrium, however, for the common congenital heart malformations or for schizophrenia and it is surprising that selection has not made these conditions less common. A possible explanation is that they represent one end of a process of stabilizing selection, and that balancing the selection against genes predisposing to, say, schizophrenia there is a selection against individuals who markedly deviate genetically from the population mean in the opposite deviation from patients with schizophrenia. This is plausible for example in the case of congenital dislocation of the hip, a congenital malformation where one of the mechanisms concerned in the genetic predisposition is known. This is a tendency to develop a shallow acetabular socket to the hip joint. An unduly deep acetabulum, which would be a mild form of protrusio acetabuli, or Otto's pelvis, would also be disadvantageous.

Mutation is relatively unimportant for the birth frequency with this stabilizing selection. Its effect is likely to be just to increase the genetic variance and this will be contained by the selection against both extremes. Most of the genetic variation in the system is due to mendelian segregation. The principle is shown in Figure 1.3 where it is assumed that genetic variation is first due to two alleles of equal frequency at each of two loci, *a* and *b* giving low values and *a′* and *b′* high values. Thus *aabb* individuals and *a′a′b′b′* individuals could each be lethal without altering the gene frequencies from generation to generation. If selection against the genes predisposing to, say, a shallow acetabulum, say *a* and *b*, is relaxed because the condition is readily treated if detected in the neonatal period, but there is no corresponding relaxation of the counterselection, it is to be expected that the population mean and the distribution will shift in the direction of a shallow acetabulum since the genes *a′* and *b′* are still being eliminated. This would lead to an increase in the birth frequency of the congenital anomaly.

Any estimates of the increase in birth frequency from new treatments in such a situation can only be guesses, but some indication of the size of the effect may be had from direct observation. In the case of infantile pyloric stenosis, which has a birth frequency of about 1 in 500, mortality in infancy until 1920 was about 0·9 (90 per cent). It was then rapidly reduced and is now about 0·01 (1 per cent) in good centres and perhaps 0·05 over-all in Britain. It has been shown that about 4 per cent of the children of survivors

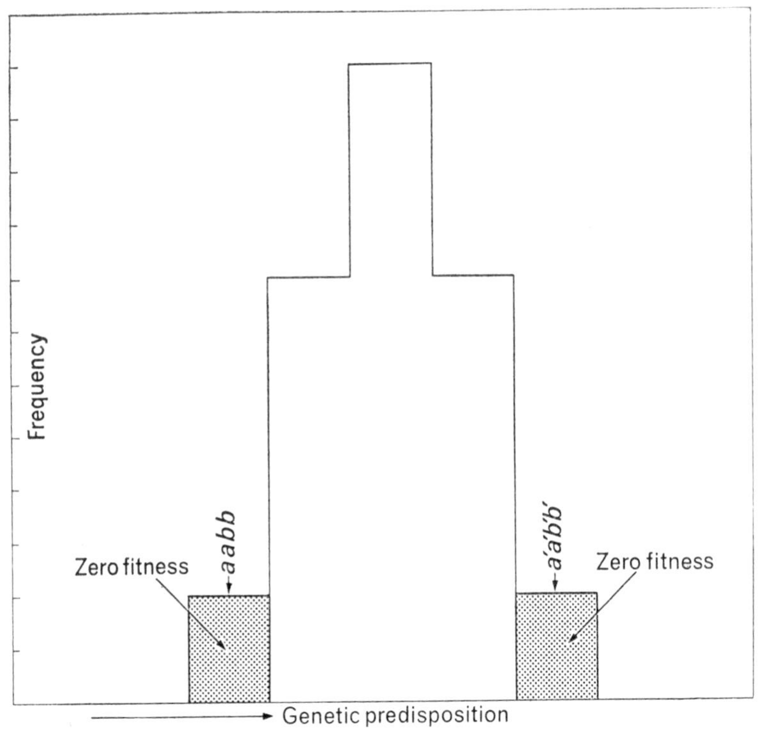


**Figure 1.3**

of the condition are affected, and most of these children would not have been born if their parents had not been treated. In a 30-year-old series no patient had a proven affected parent. In a more recent series already 3 per cent of patients were born to a parent who had been treated in infancy. Looking at the problem more theoretically on the simplest assumption of polygenic inheritance and assuming a heritability of some 70 per cent, the birth frequency is now likely to rise by some 3 per cent in each generation, which would give a doubling of the birth frequency in some 25 generations. The underlying genetic change could, however, be masked by a lessening of the strength of the unknown environmental factors. In the case of those congenital heart malformations, which are being successfully treated by surgery and would have been lethal in childhood, the proportion of offspring affected is not yet established, but is probably on average rather less than with pyloric stenosis, perhaps 3 per cent, and the rise in birth frequency might be about 2 per cent per generation. This, other things being equal, would give a doubling in some 35 generations. On the same simple assumptions, the rate of increase in frequency from such treatments will be related to initial population frequency. With a condition as common as schizophrenia, affecting about 1 per cent of the population, and assuming a heritability of about 70 per cent, the rate of increase will be about 5 per cent per generation, giving a doubling in a little more than twenty generations. If schizophrenia was determined by a mutant gene such that only about 1 in 5 of heterozygotes had the disease, and the gene was maintained in the population by an increased reproductive fitness of those heterozygotes who were clinically unaffected, the rise following new treatments which substantially raised the fitness of patients but did not modify the advantage of clinically unaffected heterozygotes would be more rapid, it would still, however, imply a doubling time of about seven generations.

## Doubling times

The times taken for birth frequencies to double following the introduction of an effective new treatment raising fitness from zero to 0·9 and assuming no countermeasures are taken are approximately as follows:

| | |
|---|---|
| Mongolism | 3 generations (or 5 if male patients do not transmit) |
| Dominant conditions | 1 generation |
| Recessive conditions | 150 generations, unless persistent heterozygote advantage |
| X-linked conditions | 5 generations |
| Polygenic conditions | 25 generations, if birth frequency 0·3 per cent<br>20 generations, if birth frequency 1·0 per cent |

## Eugenic countermeasures

It is unlikely that the birth frequencies of genetically and part-genetically determined conditions will be allowed to rise substantially as a result of the introduction of new treatment. The coming of the planned small family, and widespread if rather imprecise knowledge of human genetics in the general population, is bringing a feeling of responsibility on the part of parents for the genetic health of their children. This had lead to an increasing demand for genetic counselling and couples are already showing a marked interest in prenatal screening procedures for abnormalities even before these are available in practice. With this good will on the part of their patients, a genetically well-educated and vigorous medical profession will, I think, be able, without exerting any undue pressure, to guide parental choice in a way that will not only prevent any increase in disease from new methods of treatment, but often lower the birth frequency below the present equilibrium level.

As regards chromosal disorders there is no present danger of any increase in birth frequency from effective new treatments. Further, prenatal diagnosis of chromosomal anomalies by culturing amniotic cells offers the prospect of substantially reducing the birth frequency of such anomalies where the mother wishes for a termination if a major anomaly is found. There is much need for technical development in this field; improved methods of amniocentesis permitting earlier recovery of amniotic cells (at present the optimum is 12–14 weeks after conception), quicker growth of cells (at present up to 3 weeks), and computerized screening of karyotypes. At present the technique of prenatal screening is mostly being used only in the rare cases where it is known that the mother (or her husband) carries a balanced chromosome anomaly, which will give a high risk of an unbalanced anomaly in the foetus. The logical extension, when techniques permit, is to mothers over the age of 40, who are about 2 per cent of all mothers but produce nearly 1 in 6 of mongol children. The next extension, some years ahead, is to all mothers over the age of 35 who are about 9 per cent of mothers and who produce nearly a third of all mongol children. The procedure would not be carried out unless the parents agree that they wish for a termination if a major anomaly is found, but there are already indications that many parents would welcome such a screening procedure. The expense of maintaining a severely mentally retarded child is such that the procedure is probably already an economic proposition for mothers over the age of 40 years, though sufficient laboratory facilities are not yet available. The extension of the procedure to all pregnancies is perhaps a century away; but once this is achieved no parents in an advanced community need have a child with a major chromosome anomaly. Though some to whom abortion is repugnant may well choose not to make use of the opportunity of prenatal screening.

As regards conditions determined by mutant genes, only with dominant conditions is there any likelihood of a rapid rise following new treatments. If, however, those who are successfully treated are told of the 1 in 2 risk to their children many, with serious conditions, will decide to have no children. In their case selection is as intense as if they had died in infancy. Provided overall such patients plan families well below replacement rate no considerable rise in birth frequencies of the condition will occur. Further, genetic and technical advances may again make it possible to allow such individuals to have unaffected children, but to offer a termination if the foetus is affected. Either biochemical methods or close linkages to common markers may make prenatal diagnosis possible. For example, the gene locus for dystrophia myotonica is closely linked to the secretor gene locus and the secretor gene is probably detectable in amniotic fluid. With full use of genetic counselling all cases of dominant conditions except those due to new mutations, can be prevented.

With recessive conditions genetic counselling only of those successfully treated has not much to offer. The children will almost all be normal and so the patient will not feel that he or she should not have children. However, genetic counselling of parents of affected children can reduce the number of second cases in a family. In these days of small families these are not more than a sixth of the whole. Nevertheless this in itself would be sufficient to prevent an increase following a new successful treatment of a rare recessive condition. In the future such selection through parents will be less, in that in many instances prenatal diagnosis will make it possible for parents who have had one affected child to plan more children on the understanding the pregnancy will be screened. The development of tests for the heterozygous carriers will make it possible to do more. It will make it possible to test the fiancées of successfully treated patients. If these are heterozygotes the marriage may not take place and if it does, prenatal screening may be used to reduce the number of affected children born. Such screening for carriers, as techniques become available, may be introduced to ascertain all carriers of the genes for certain common recessive conditions, for example, in Britain, cystic fibrosis. Some 1 in 20 individuals carry the gene for this condition and they might conveniently be ascertained at school age. Such ascertainment accompanied by prenatal diagnosis offers the hope ultimately of preventing the birth of all affected children and achieving a gradual reduction in the gene frequency.

With X-linked recessive conditions the main discovery needed to prevent any increase, following the introduction of a successful new treatment of affected males, is a way of separating X- and Y-bearing sperm. An affected male can safely have sons who will not be affected, and who will not transmit the condition, but his daughters will always be carriers and at risk of transmitting the condition to their sons. The discovery of means of separating the two types of sperm will be made much simpler by the new discovery that the Y-bearing chromosomes may be identified by fluorescent staining. The success of any separation method may, therefore, now be estimated directly *in vitro* and not by breeding experiments. Ultimately with the discovery of tests for female carriers and of methods of prenatal diagnosis all X-linked conditions will be preventable except those due to fresh mutations in ova.

With conditions due to more complex inheritance the prevention of an increase following new treatments will depend on better understanding of the mechanisms involved. At present successfully treated patients may be told of the risks to children. Most of these risks, however, unlike those associated with conditions due to mutant genes of large effect, are only moderate risks of the order of 3–5 per cent, and so will only occasionally lead to family limitation. In some instances, however, prenatal diagnosis by direct inspection of the foetus may be helpful. In the case of neural tube malformations, and in other major externally visible malformations, the procedure of direct foetoscopy is perhaps already justified where a woman has already had two affected children (risk of malformation about 1 in 8) and an experienced practitioner is available. As instruments, techniques, and experience improve the procedure may be justified where the woman or her husband is a successfully treated patient. Unfotunately there appears to be no immediate prospects of prenatal diagnosis of congenital heart malformations. Further, once the genetic mechanisms maintaining some of the serious common diseases at relatively high frequency in the population are better understood, it may be possible to prevent increases in the frequencies of these disorders following new treatments by more indirect methods. For example, if stabilizing selection is in fact operating, it may be possible to prevent any increase by simultaneously overcoming the reduced fitness at the other end of the distribution of the genetic predisposition. For example, if the 'diabetic' genotype was, as has been suggested, a 'thrifty' genotype enabling survival under conditions of near starvation, the absence of recurrent famines and sieges may be tending to reduce the frequency of individuals with a marked genetic predisposition to diabetes at the same time as treatment of frank diabetes is tending to increase the frequency.

In the long term when dealing with conditions due to the extremes of normal genetic variation some thought must be given to priorities and the gravity of different forms of relaxation of selection. The size of jaws and teeth has fallen steadily since man first made flint knives. Communities that have for long depended on agriculture have lower average visual acuity, and a higher incidence of colour blindness, than populations still at a hunting and gathering stage of economy. The reduction in childhood mortality from infection will tend to gradually reduce the mean genetic endowment for the development of cellular and humoral immunity. While some of these trends may not be important, in general it would seem wise for human populations to attempt to maintain a high degree of genetic variability, so that environmental changes may be met without too much morbidity.

# 2

# Predicting the long-term effects of treating inherited disease: some comments

H. HARRIS
MD, FRS
*Galton Professor of Human Genetics*
*University College London*

# Predicting the long-term effects of treating inherited disease: some comments

It has often been argued that advances in medicine by leading to a relaxation of natural selection are resulting in the progressive accumulation of deleterious genes in human populations, so that eventually the species will collapse under the burden of its genetic load. This extreme view is often based on a somewhat naïve and very simplistic idea of the mode of operation of natural selection and on an underestimation of the genetic complexity of human populations. I do not think that present advances in our understanding and treatment of inherited disorders require this grave prognostication of doom. When we talk about advances in medicine we are not merely talking about the treatment of specific conditions; we are also talking about understanding what disease is all about and how to cope with it. Genetic counselling, palliative treatments, therapeutic abortion, the modification of social conditions, and so on, are all parts of this advance and have to be taken into account in considering the future. The human species may well succeed in destroying itself in the not too distant future, but if so it is likely to be by other means and for very different reasons.

Nevertheless the prediction of what changes in the genetical structure of human populations may occur in the future as the result of current changes in the physical and social conditions of life and of the advances in medical care presents a number of real and difficult problems.

In large part the difficulties arise from our ignorance of the precise basis of the genetical predisposition of many common diseases and other abnormalities which appear to have a multifactorial aetiology. Diseases such as schizophrenia and diabetes, for example, apparently depend on both genetic and environmental causes but as yet we have virtually no idea of the precise functions or of the incidence of the particular genes involved, and also little notion of the particular facets in the environment which elicit these diseases in predisposed individuals. The elucidation of such problems could well lead to quite rapid changes in the incidence of these conditions by allowing us to alter in a specific way the nature of the environment to which predisposed individuals are exposed. Changes of this sort may also be expected to lead to alterations in the genetic structure of the population, because as the selective pressures change the gene frequencies will progressively alter so that the population tends to become more adjusted to the new situation. But such genetic changes will be relatively slow, and even further environmental changes may well have come about before a new equilibrium has been reached.

There have been, of course, during the last few generations, considerable changes in the physical and social conditions in which human populations live. And it is therefore quite possible that many of the gene frequencies which occur today do not represent genetic equilibria in the classical sense. This clearly makes prediction much more difficult. For example, the recessive disease, cystic fibrosis of the pancreas, has an incidence much higher than might be expected, and one explanation that has been put forward for this is that the heterozygote enjoys, or enjoyed in the past, some kind of selective advantage relative to the normal homozygote. But if this is so and one wants to predict what may happen in the future, it is obviously important to find out what the nature of such a selective advantage may actually be and whether conditions which might have produced it in the past and led to the high incidence still exist today.

The alteration in selective pressure due to the introduction of an effective therapy for a particular inherited disease is in general likely to cause a much more rapid change in the frequency of genes determining dominantly inherited disorders where the affected individuals are heterozygotes, than of genes determining recessively inherited disorders where the affected patients are homozygous. The selective pressure against a particular gene is measured by the relative contribution that individuals carrying it make in offspring to the next generation. And it is perhaps important to remember that some dominant disorders, while they may cause quite a considerable degree of morbidity, may not be associated with a corresponding reduction in biological fitness as measured in terms of their number of offspring.

Huntington's chorea, for example, is a severe disease of middle life, and is not excessively uncommon. Its incidence is thought to be about 1 in 20,000 in the adult population and since it generally does not become manifest until the middle 30s or later, the patients have often completed their families before it appears. Many of the children at present well, will sooner or later develop the disease. Thus, perhaps 5,000 or more individuals in the country today suffer from the condition or will do so later. But in general their contribution of genes to the next generation appears to be only marginally limited, if at all. So the development of an effective treatment for this disease, while it would constitute a major advance in public health, would not be likely to lead to any rapid spread of the abnormal gene.

A feature of many recessive diseases which has some interesting implications in the present context, is that they often differ quite markedly in incidence from one population to another. For example, among Jewish people whose ancestors come from an area round the Baltic, the incidence of heterozygotes for a gene which in homozygotes gives rise to Tay Sachs disease appears to be about 2–3 per cent, whereas in other populations the gene is about one-tenth as frequent. Because the incidence of the disease is a function of the square of the gene frequency this means that the disorder is about one hundred times as common in these particular Jewish populations than elsewhere. But as population intermixture, which is no doubt occurring to a greater extent than in the past and will probably increase even more in the future, goes on, the population frequency of the gene will fall by dilution and the incidence of disease will be progressively reduced.

Similar gene frequency differences are to be found between much larger population groups. For example, the frequency of the gene determining phenylketonuria appears to be considerably higher in people of European origin than in Negroes. On the other hand the gene for sickle-cell anaemia is very much more common among Negroes. Similarly the incidence of genes determining fibrocystic disease of the pancreas appears to be very much higher among Europeans than among Asians or Negroes. Racial intermixture may be expected to reduce progressively the frequency of such genes and hence the incidence of the particular disorders. And such effects are likely to take place much more rapidly than any increase in the gene frequencies which might be brought about by effective treatment of individuals with these disorders. Indeed, advocates of positive eugenics might well consider the merits of a policy of racial intermixture. It would be a change from the now discredited concept of racial purity and it might well result in other long-term social advantages. It would certainly reduce the incidence of many rare recessive disorders.

However, even if we accept the view that eugenic considerations need not deter us from developing and applying new therapies for inherited diseases, there still remains the problem round which this symposium is mainly oriented. This is simply that the cost of a widespread application of many of the advances in medical technology is becoming formidable, so that the question of priorities will arise in situations where resources are limited. Even in the relatively simple case of phenylketonuria it is clear that for effective treatment to have a chance, it is necessary to establish quite an elaborate organization for screening all newborn infants at birth in order to pick out those affected, and the treatment itself is expensive and requires among other things long-term laboratory control. Similar problems are likely to arise as advances in other conditions are made, and *in toto* the financial requirements and the use of skilled personnel in maintaining such programmes will certainly be very large. The important point, however, is that such considerations are essentially the same whether one is considering inherited diseases or other conditions.

# DISCUSSION

*Progress in medicine is usually bought at a price—sometimes a steep one—and improved medical techniques for the treatment of genetically determined disorders are no exception. Most of these new treatments offer survival but not cure. Many patients are enabled to lead independent, active, and useful lives, but remain a continuing charge on the medical services of the community. Others survive to lead more circumscribed lives and they will be dependent on their fellow citizens for protection and support as well as for medical care. Moreover, longer and more active survival, often in the community instead of in an institution—brings greater opportunities for reproduction to a group of people, some of whom are likely to prove inadequate parents and many of whom will have children who in their turn will become a charge on the medical and social services of the community.*

*The geneticists, with their long-term view of coming generations, seemed to be less uneasy about this predicament than the clinicians, who are already coping with the practical difficulties of the situation and look forward with some apprehension to its possible aggravation in the future. The geneticists, with what their colleagues thought to be misplaced complacency, considered that time is on our side and that any increase in these disorders will be so slow that we shall be able to mount effective countermeasures. For this defence they rely chiefly on genetic counselling and on more sensitive techniques for identifying before birth, or even before conception, the poor risk, the chromosomal anomaly, the likelihood of malformation.*

*Obviously the more firm facts and the more practical help that can be offered, the more parents will be likely to ask for counsel. Again, the more surely the pattern of the small family is established, the more anxious parents will be that their children should be of good quality. But at present it is estimated that only 1 in 10 families who need advice seek it, and doctors who practise at some distance from a teaching hospital or specialist centre might well set the figure even lower. Both counselling and prenatal screening are expensive and the community will have to decide how much of its resources it is prepared to set aside for this work. The results of prevention are often intangible, but the admittedly heavy cost of, for instance, carrying out amnioncentesis on all elderly primiparae must be balanced against the cost of looking after a patient with Down's syndrome, who is now likely to live to a fairly ripe old age.*

*Contraception and voluntary sterilization are other safeguards against the spread of hereditary disorders. But forcible sterilization would be unacceptable, and some of the people for whom the procedure might suitably be recommended will be unable themselves to make a meaningful decision, while others may be unwilling to agree. Another genetic hazard of which medical progress is the involuntary originator is the limitation of the gene's chance to adapt to new circumstances. The interplay of genes and environment has made us such as we are, and a high mortality was an important instrument in achieving adaptation to modified surroundings. By sharply reducing the death-rate we have removed this possibly blunt, but effective, instrument, and at a time when the environment is changing more rapidly than ever before, we have more or less imposed stability on the helpless gene.*

*Further advances in knowledge—and genetics is a growing point of medicine—may solve some of these problems (and no doubt create fresh ones). But for the present the clinicians felt that though the geneticists have defined the threat of genetical hazards with mathematical precision, their proposed countermeasures are disappointingly vague and their time-scale over-optimistic.*

# The maintenance of the helpless idiot

L. S. PENROSE
MA, MD, DSc, FRCP, FRS
*Research Director*
*Kennedy–Galton Centre for*
*Mental Retardation Research and Diagnosis*

# The maintenance of the helpless idiot

In considering the problems concerning the maintenance of the severely mentally handicapped at the present time, it may be useful to inquire about what has been done in the past so that the correct perspective can be obtained. In western civilizations the history of organized care for idiots, as they were formerly termed, began rather more than a hundred years ago. In France, although great improvements were introduced in the care of the mentally ill early last century, the recognition that idiots presented a special problem (as expounded by Esquirol and Seguin) did not come until about the middle of the century, as was also the case in England. Before this, severely handicapped patients (idiots and imbeciles), when they could not be looked after at home, were admitted to general mental hospitals, to workhouses or, if they were lucky, to convents or monasteries. Typical of the new developments was the campaign of the Revd Andrew Reed, in consequence of whose energy and initiative schools and institutions were built and financed with charitable support. The object was to provide relief for parents and, at the same time, to make the patients happy while they would be educated and trained so that they could take part, as far as possible, in ordinary life. If the patients were helpless or ineducable they would be cared for in the hospitals indefinitely if the parents or relatives so wished.

It was soon found by some of the most enthusiastic reformers that there were no easy methods available for improving the lot of the idiot. Nurses and teachers had to work very hard without achieving any appreciable objective improvements in the conditions of their patients. Deterioration was commoner than advancement. The staffs of the institutions were largely composed of dedicated and conscientious people who took pleasure in doing their best to make their patients comfortable. It is important to realize that, almost universally, mentally defective patients are friendly and appreciative in sharp contrast to the majority of inmates of the hospitals for chronic psychotics. Thus good personal relationships are easily maintained between staff and patients in mental subnormality hospitals which compensate, to some extent, for the disappointing results of many of their educative efforts.

After a period of some fifty years or so, most of the institutions, which had begun as charities, became largely the concern of local authorities and many large hospitals were built entirely at public expense to house the increasing numbers of patients of low mental grade who were recognized to need special care over long periods. Perhaps inevitably there was a public reaction of disapproval which gradually developed. The idea grew in many people's minds that too much money was being spent on a hopeless task. At the beginning of the present century, in parallel with enthusiasm for eugenics which developed in the USA, there was a demand in many quarters in this country for legislation which would enable the number of the mentally defective to be controlled by sterilization or even by euthanasia. It was a commonly held view that the parents of idiots were in some way mentally handicapped themselves. In spite of repeated demonstrations that this was not the case, it was not until the monstrous excesses of the Nazi regime appeared in Germany that demands for sterilization as a remedy became entirely unpopular.

At the present time, the public view of mental subnormality has undergone another change which, as before, is based to a considerable extent upon ignorance. The nature of mental illness is generally much better understood than that of mental deficiency. The distinction between the two types of disease was established in England by law in 1300 but it was abolished by the Mental Health Act of 1959. The concept of mental disorder now covers both insanity and subnormality. It was widely believed, about ten years ago, that, in consequence of advances in the treatment of psychoses by tranquillizing drugs, it should be soon possible to reduce significantly the number of mental hospital beds. In hospitals for the subnormal where the discharge rates did not immediately rise, the staffs were thought to be neglecting their patients and their work was spoken of with derision in the public press and even in official quarters. Let us now consider some of the facts concerning the patients in these hospitals, their ages, sexes, mental grades, and expectations of life.

Some forty years ago when I began a survey of patients at the Royal Eastern Counties' Institution at Colchester, about half of them were of the idiot or imbecile grade, that is severely subnormal in modern terminology. There has been a trend for many years to admit a greater proportion of helpless cases than formerly. This can be clearly shown by comparing figures compiled after an interval of many years. A survey of patients at Harperbury Hospital recently showed that about three-quarters of them were in the severely subnormal category. The trend is emphasized by the increasing life-span of idiots and imbeciles under present-day environmental conditions and medical techniques. For example, mongolism, or Down's syndrome, comprised only 1 or 2 per cent of resident patients in 1900; the figure had risen to 5 per cent in 1930 and the disorder now accounts for about 10 per cent which constitutes a fivefold rise in seventy years. These patients formerly had a very high mortality rate, especially from tuberculosis, but now, provided that they survive early infancy, are not unhealthy. Their expectation of life at birth has increased from 8 to 9 years in 1930 to nearly 20 years at the present time. Correspondingly, the mean age of Down's patients among hospital residents has gradually increased and is now reported to be about 28 years. In association with these changes, improvements in life expectancy have affected almost all groups of patients. Whereas the mean age of patients at Colchester was less than 25 years, that reported at Lennox Castle and St Lawrence's Hospital recently is nearly 40 years. Even for the low-grade and helpless cases the span of life has increased and some 5 per cent of them are reported to live to be over 50 years. It is most important to appreciate that severely handicapped and helpless patients are by no means always children, as is often imagined. In fact the majority of idiots who require care are adults. Imbeciles indeed can live to a great age, even to over 90 years. In the early age-groups it is common to find an excess of male severely subnormal cases but, among the more elderly, females predominate.

The clinical problems of these patients must now be discussed in relation to the prospects of treatment or prevention. The total population incidence of all types of severe subnormality is about

1 in 400, of whom less than half are cared for outside their own homes. The incidence at birth is far higher than 1 in 400 because many types of severe malformation, which would inevitably imply gross mental disability, such as anencephaly, are incompatible with survival. Of the survivors, about 1 in 10 are Down's syndrome but there are also a few cases of other sorts of chromosomal errors of a variety of types. The hereditary biochemical defects, like phenylketonuria, are rarer but there are slightly more numerous hereditary cases of different kinds, true microcephales, epiloiacs, and neurological diseases. Specific illnesses of environmental origin, birth injuries, results of maternal incompatibility, or infections like rubella and childhood meningitis and encephalitis only account for a small percentage of cases, perhaps 5 per cent. For the rest, probably in more than half the cases we have no indication of the cause though, in some instances, an eponymous diagnosis is made, as in the syndrome of de Lange.

With regard to treatment, a few rare biochemical conditions have been found to respond favourably, phenylketonuria and homocystinuria, for example, but no modern methods have made any noticeable impact on the great mass of cases. Congenital syphilis, indeed, has disappeared but therapeutics applied to tuberculous meningitis saved some patients who have become defective but who would otherwise have died. Treatment can physically relieve hydrocephalus and some cases of spastic diplegia but the mental effects are not striking. Fortunately, more can be said now of the possibilities of prevention in hereditary groups than could have been a decade ago. In particular, there are new hopes for reducing the prevalence of Down's syndrome, first by avoidance of pregnancies at late maternal ages, secondly by advice to avoid risks when a parent has a D/G or G/G translocation and, thirdly, by amniocentesis examinations in critical cases where the risk is known to be high.

I now come to the more immediate problem of how these patients are best cared for. In the whole country there are beds available for some 50,000 of them, if we include private institutions. The original idea, a century ago, was to take them away from their own homes when the parents were not able to give them sufficient attention and provide nursing care and educational facilities of an elementary kind. A popular view, however, is that they are kept away from their own homes against their better interests, that they pine for their parents and are neglected physically and educationally. The truth lies, of course, in an intermediate position. The subnormality hospitals are understaffed and overcrowded and in some the medical and educational facilities are unsatisfactory. However, the problem of optimal treatment is no simple one.

As already mentioned, the patients are mostly adults and they suffer from a large variety of diseases. It is less easy to evoke popular sentiment about the needs of adult imbeciles than about those of children. Children are admitted to children's wards but, after ten or twenty years, the same patients may still be there, mentally still children or infants but chronologically adult. It used to be said that the patients remained technically children until they were moved to the old people's wards at about the age of 50. Then, there is the question of what used to be called 'cot and chair' cases as opposed to the rest. Completely helpless patients require continual nursing and feeding as well. With adults this involves much physical exertion. Patients who can walk and feed themselves can usually be taught to be moderately clean in their habits and are comparatively easy to manage. They live comfortable vegetative lives in hospital and are easy to entertain, especially now that television is universal.

How far is it a practical proposition for any of these patients to live at home instead of in hospital? The present-day situation concerning housing with small flats and no domestic help is very different from the quiet rural surroundings in which imbeciles can flourish. It is becoming increasingly difficult for severely mentally handicapped patients to be looked after in their own homes and there is no escape from the prospect of having to plan to care for a very large proportion of them out of public funds. There are, however, alternative methods. The hospitals can be large or small, the patients can be divided into groups who are suitable for different kinds of nursing or training and divided up also by age and sex. The magic word 'hostel' is often used to appeal to the public by hospital boards and indeed a hostel for adult imbeciles can be a pleasant and friendly society. On the other hand the administrative problems of hostels are much greater than those of hospitals or larger units. Small units are more difficult to staff and more expensive to run than large units. Many years ago I attended a working party to find, in theory, the optimum economic size of a mental hospital; the result was that about 1,000 beds was deemed to be most efficient. Hostels are usually units of 20–50 beds and are best suited for patients who can do a fair amount for themselves, can help in the housework and can go out to factory jobs in the most favourable instances or to sheltered workshops. These benefits cannot apply generally to the cases of severe subnormality, none of whom can be left without supervision.

If anyone thinks that modern medical science or a change in mode of administration will easily solve the problems of mental deficiency by rule of thumb, he is living in a fool's paradise. It is no use imagining that mental deficiency hospitals can be abolished as being old-fashioned without causing immense confusion, and, indeed, hardship for patients who are used to their daily television, their concerts, films, and social events. We must realize that the problems are more extensive than ever before. Probably many of them can be solved. But to do this much more knowledge is required. Scientific investigations on causes, treatment, and prevention are still urgently needed. The problems also must be more accurately explained to administrative authorities and the peculiar difficulties of this service appreciated. To use the available resources in the best possible way, full co-operation is needed between all those concerned in research and administration, in both the medical and educational fields.

## SELECTED REFERENCES

PENROSE, L. S. (1938). 'A clinical and genetic study of 1,280 cases of mental defect', *Spec Rep. Ser. Med. Res. Counc.* no. 229 (London: HMSO).

—— (1963). *Biology of Mental Defect,* 3rd edn (London: Sidgwick & Jackson).

PRIMROSE, D. A. (1966). 'Natural history of mental deficiency in a hospital group and in the community it serves', *J. ment. Defic. Res.* **10,** 159.

RICHARDS, B. W. (1970). 'Statistical analysis of the hospital population', in *Mental Subnormality: Modern Trends in Research* (London: Pitman Medical and Scientific Publishing Co. Ltd).

# 4

# The care of the profoundly retarded person

A. KUSHLICK
MRCP, DPH
*Director of Research into Subnormality*
*Wessex Regional Hospital Board*

# The care of the profoundly retarded person

MANY misconceptions exist about the so-called 'helpless idiot', and some of these affect decisions on the provision of services to look after him. The following definition illustrates the confusion. It is taken from a Penguin book, first published in 1952, and widely used by undergraduate students of many disciplines.

Idiots are wholly dependent. They cannot be taught to feed themselves, or to keep themselves clean, nor can they recognize other people or communicate with them except in the crudest and most primitive way. They are in fact considerably less intelligent than domestic animals. Their habits are simple and unformed and their emotional responses crude in the extreme. When frustrated they may bite or scratch themselves. They tend to pull out their hair and eat it. Unlike imbeciles, whose emotional state is usually readily apparent, they appear to be neither happy nor unhappy in the accepted sense of these descriptions (1).

It asserts that these people have a very poor prognosis, cannot acquire a range of basic skills, and have a combination of disagreeable and bizarre behaviour. Moreover, it asserts that such people are completely unresponsive to, or oblivious of, the quality of the environment in which they find themselves. It follows from the definition that these behaviours are inherent and that nothing can, or needs to, be done to modify them. It goes on to assert that these phenomena are found in all people with IQ scores below the level of 20.

The evidence, however, shows that most children and adults who cannot even score at all on formal IQ tests, can do many of the things that the definition asserts they cannot, that a very small minority are completely immobile or have the bizarre behaviours supposedly found in all, that virtually none are completely unresponsive to the quality of the environment in which they find themselves, and that the majority are capable of a repertoire of behaviour easily recognizable as indicating happiness or dejection. In our detailed studies of every severely subnormal (SSN—IQ under 50) child generated by a total population of 400,000 we have not come across a single child who would fit into the criteria of the above definition. On the contrary, the majority appear so 'normal' physically, biochemically, and cytogenetically, that the diagnosis (unlike Down's syndrome or PKU) cannot at present be made until well after birth. In the most skilled hands, at the present time, predictions of the abilities in later life of infants or young children carry a high risk of error (2).

In addition, evidence is accumulating that, not only are the profoundly retarded capable of learning new behaviours, but also that some of their bizarre behaviours may have been acquired from routines of child rearing practised at home or in understaffed institutions which have acted as unplanned, but effective, reinforcement schedules for these behaviours. There is now a growing literature on operant conditioning or behaviour modification with evidence, some from well-controlled trials, of the effectiveness of these techniques both in extinguishing the bizarre behaviours that may have developed, and for building up new behaviour repertoires. The techniques developed for observing systematically the behaviour of the children and for programming the teaching of new skills may well make important contributions to the study of child development and child rearing, and to the teaching of children with a much wider range of learning difficulties (3).

Profound retardation occurs rarely and the available evidence suggests that the incidence (inception rate of new cases) and, indeed, the prevalence (rate of existing cases) among children has remained constant for the past ten years. Indeed, there is no evidence that advances in medical care or other changes affecting infant and childhood mortality have seriously increased the prevalence of severe or profound subnormality among children since the classical survey of England and Wales undertaken by E. O. Lewis in 1927 (4). This was first reported by Goodman and Tizard in 1962 (5). The prevalence of children with an IQ of under 50 in Britain at ages 7–19 is now about 3·65 per 1,000. Lewis's rates

**Table 4.1**

| | *Wessex 1963* | *England and Wales 1927* |
|---|---|---|
| Children | 14—Non-ambulant or severely incontinent<br>+9—Severely behaviour-disordered | 13—IQ under 20 |
| Adults | 33—Unable to speak in sentences or to feed, wash and dress themselves | 17—IQ under 20 |

in 1927 were 3·76 and 5·14 per 1,000 in urban and rural areas respectively. The prevalence of mongolism has risen from 0·1 per 1,000 in 1927 to 1·1 per 1,000 in the 1960s, largely as a result of increased survival, but the prevalence of non-mongol children, among whom are most of the profoundly retarded, has fallen. There are some problems of comparability of these data (6).

The absence of exactly comparable data makes it difficult to assess changes in prevalence among the profoundly handicapped over this period. Lewis's rates for children of IQ under 20 were 0·74 and 1·32 per 1,000 for urban and rural areas respectively. Rates from Wessex in 1963 (7) were 1·13 per 1,000 for SSN people aged 15–19 who were unable to speak in sentences or to feed, wash, and dress themselves without help (many could do one or more, but not all of these things).

Table 4.1 compares, in so far as it is possible, the crude rates per 100,000 total population of profound handicap found in Wessex in 1963 with those found by Lewis in 1927.

Both comparisons appear to show rises in prevalence since 1927. The comparability of rates among children is less reliable than among adults. However, there is additional evidence of a real rise in rates among adults, due to falling death-rates among children (8). Results from Wessex show a rise in SSN adult prevalence between 1963 and 1967. However, this rise occurs mainly among the most able of these adults. There is no change in the rates for the most profoundly retarded.

The rates per 100,000 total population for institutional care of the SSN (IQ under 50) child appear actually to have fallen between 1927 and 1963. No separate figures are available for SSN adults in 1927, but the over-all rates for all grades of institutionalized mentally handicapped adults have also fallen since 1927. These figures are shown in Table 4.2.

**Table 4.2.** *Crude rates per 100,000 total population among those receiving institutional care in 1927 and 1963.*

| | *Wessex 1963* | *England and Wales 1927* |
|---|---|---|
| SSN children | 18 (5 non-ambulant) | 22·1 (6 non-ambulant) |
| SSN and MSN adults | 134 | 189 |

It is of interest that the rates recommended for institutional provision in 1927, the middle of the eugenic era in which predictions of rapid and dramatic increases in prevalence were made, are nearly double the rates now recommended on the basis of recent prevalence surveys.

Table 4.3 shows the staff currently available to meet the institutional needs of the existing numbers of mentally subnormal people of all grades in hospital (9).

**Table 4.3.** *Number of staff and residents in hospitals for the mentally subnormal on any weekday per consultant-in-subnormality: (a) In the fourteen hospitals with the lowest nurse/resident ratio ('Low'). (b) In the seven hospitals with the highest nurse/resident ratio ('High').*

| | *'Low'* | | *'High'* | |
|---|---|---|---|---|
| Consultant | 1 | | 1 | |
| Other doctor | 1·39 | | 1·46 | |
| Psychologist | 0·45 | | 0·39 | |
| Social worker | 0·33 | | 0·32 | |
| Therapist | 2·0 | | 2·25 | |
| Industrial therapist | 1·89 | | 0·14 | |
| Qualified teachers | 0·94 | 4·22 | 0·82 | 4·82 |
| Other teachers | 3·44 | | 4·0 | |
| Qualified nurses* | 12·3 | 31·9 | 12·0 | 41·9 |
| Other nurses* | 19·6 | | 29·9 | |
| Ward orderlies | 5·6 | | 6·2 | |
| Residents | 555 | | 357 | |
| | i.e. approx. 600 | 80 SSN children<br>320 SSN adults<br>200 MSN adults | i.e. approx. 300 | 40 SSN children<br>160 SSN adults<br>100 MSN adults |
| Total population served (to nearest 100,000) | 400,000 | | 200,000 | |
| Approximate number of mentally handicapped living at home | 820 | 320 SSN children<br>200 SSN adults<br>300 MSN adults | 410 | 160 SSN children<br>100 SSN adults<br>150 MSN adults |

*Ratios at any time of the day estimated from over-all staff/resident ratio.

This shows that in 'Low' hospitals (including the largest and most prestigious hospitals for the mentally subnormal) 32 nurses, 4 teachers, 3 therapists, and 2 industrial trainers wait for decisions on nearly 600 patients by one consultant. He is helped by 0·44 psychologists and 0·32 social workers.

This paper also shows that these staffing levels set severe limits on the quality of care possible in these hospitals and that the resulting management routines may, indeed, produce iatrogenic disabilities among the inmates. The weekly cost per resident in these hospitals has recently risen from about £14 to £20 per week.

The standards of resources obtaining in hospitals for the mentally handicapped have been systematically reviewed by Dr Pauline Morris (10).

## Family problems

The problems experienced by the families of SSN children and adults living at home have now been well documented by Tizard and Grad (11) and by others. These problems arise both from the complex logistic problems of caring in a busy household for a child whose physical growth exceeds the expected rate of social development, and from the unhelpful and often conflicting advice given to the family by different medical and social-work practitioners. In an evaluation of new forms of residential care for mentally handicapped children, we are measuring these problems as well as those arising in relation to the institutionalizing of the child—before, during, and after the admission procedure.

The evidence of all studies, however, confirms that parents are interested in their children and anxious to play their part whenever possible in the care of their children. The complexities in organization of the services are confusing to parents and professionals alike, and the lack of time and knowledge on the part of some of the key medical and social work personnel tend to negative the possible parental contribution to the child's care. Visiting frequency among families with children in hospital has been shown to be related to the distance they live from the hospital. It is likely that it is also affected by visiting rules and regulations. We have found evidence of administrative procedures which actively discourage parental participation.

## The severely subnormal and the over-all problem of chronic handicap

The problem of the severely (including the profoundly) retarded is but a small part of the major problem of chronic handicapping conditions. Although these have existed for many years, they are only now beginning to be recognized as a major problem of mainstream medical care, education, and research.

Compared with other chronic handicapping conditions—for example, those among the elderly—the whole problem of the profoundly or severely retarded is relatively small. The elderly, who constitute only 12–13 per cent of the total population, occupy about 40 per cent of psychiatric and 42 per cent of non-psychiatric hospital places.

**Table 4.4.** *Total population 100,000.*

| | | |
|---|---|---|
| ELDERLY (aged 65+) | | |
| Bedfast | 350 | (220)* |
| Confined to home | 1,410 | (1,300) |
| Mobile outside with difficulty | 1,020 | (910) |
| None of above | 9,240 | (9,100) |
| MENTALLY SUBNORMAL (all ages) | | |
| Non-ambulant | 21 | (8) |
| Severe behaviour problems | 31 | (7) |
| Severely incontinent | 14 | (4) |
| None of above | 247 | (142) |

*Figures in parentheses show those living at home.

Table 4.4 illustrates the size and nature of these two problems by comparing the prevalence of different types of handicap to be found in a total population of 100,000 (12). The figures for the mentally handicapped include the severely subnormal (including the profoundly subnormal) and the mildly subnormal.

## Conclusions

In what way is the presence of the profoundly retarded acting against the interest of the other groups 'sick' or 'well', who make up society? Is there a case for redistributing to these other groups resources now available to the profoundly retarded and to the doctors working with them?

My own answer to both questions is no.

On the one hand, I believe that pressure for any resources the profoundly handicapped are now receiving and, in particular, any increase in resources they might in future receive, derives from the other groups in society—public opinion, government, and to a minor extent special interest lobbies.

Moreover, evidence for the harmful effects on society produced by the profoundly handicapped is more often characterized by lack of information than by its rigour. Problems arising from the manner in which the profoundly retarded and their families are treated, or from the way in which their facilities have been developed and maintained have become associated with the handicapped people themselves. Thus, impressions of their unsightliness often arise from institutional clothing policies of bulk-buying of out-of-date or specially designed, unfashionable clothes. The clothes are ill-fitting because lack of staff and lack of storage space on the wards necessitate sharing. They are badly finished because central linen-rooms or laundries are not equipped to provide a service of ordinary household standards—central laundries may indeed be expensively destructive of the clothing they process.

The difficulties associated with achieving a team approach to problem-solving among professionals of the different disciplines involved arise from the apparently arbitrary way in which different components of continuing care have been segmented by the historical development of the services and what have been defined collectively as the 'caring' professions. The dislocation of the institutionalized handicapped and the professionals involved in their care from their base communities has arisen from the policy of siting these facilities in large complexes necessarily distant from the population centres in which the residents' families live.

It seems likely that our failure as a profession to begin solving these problems has generated a pessimism which prevents us from focusing attention on the main problems, i.e., the learning problems of people with handicaps and the associated long-term and complex problems of their families.

Looked at on the basis of administrative areas of 100,000 total population, the problem looks much simpler than for populations of 500,000 or a million. Solutions to the problems of care also look much simpler if the number of hands available to participate are increased. We have not yet even begun to explore ways of allowing parents to collaborate in looking after their children who are in residential care, or of creating a climate of opinion and administrative structure to allow ordinary citizens to contribute to the care of their children.

The problem of evaluating medical care by examining the coverage and effectiveness of the service for those who receive it is complex. Methods for doing so need to be developed. The problem of severe subnormality or profound retardation is small enough and rich enough in its diversity to present a feasible pilot model for such methods.

In our studies we are finding that, far from being a bizarre specialized problem, the care of these people presents a microcosm of the major problems facing medicine today. The techniques piloted in mental retardation for measuring the size of the problem and its nature, and the criteria for measuring effectiveness of the service appear to have much more in common with other medical problems than they have differences.

The scientific study of the mentally retarded has also made tentative and modest contributions to our understanding of enzymes and human metabolism while the study of child development, learning theory, and practice is gaining from the opportunity to systematize observations and test hypotheses around the care of the retarded.

The problems of the retarded and their families are complex indeed and we are only beginning to learn a little about them. The challenge is to try and solve some of them, because valid solutions here will have many applications elsewhere. There is no evidence that their presence is making our problems any more difficult. Rather it appears that their problems are our problems. We may well have much to gain from trying to solve theirs.

## REFERENCES

1. Stafford-Clark, D. (1952). *Psychiatry Today* (Harmondsworth: Penguin Books Ltd).
2. Illingworth, R. S. (1961). *J. Child Psychol. Psychiat.* **2,** 210–15.
3. Bijou, S. W. (1968). *Paedriatric Clinics in North America,* **10,** 4, 969–87.
4. Lewis, E. O. (1929). *Report of the Mental Deficiency Committee,* part iv (London: HMSO).
5. Goodman, N., and Tizard, J. (1962). *Br. med. J.* **1,** 216–19.

6. KUSHLIK, A. (1968). 'Social problems of mental subnormality', in *Foundations of Child Psychiatry*, pp. 369–411 (Oxford: Pergamon Press).

7. —— and COX, G. R. (1967). 'International Conference on the Scientific Study of Mental Retardation, Montpellier, August' (mimeograph).

8. —— —— (1969). *Provision of Further Accommodation for the Mentally Subnormal* (Winchester: Wessex Regional Hospital Board).

9. —— (1970). *J. R. Soc. Hlth*, **90**, no. 5, 255–61.

10. MORRIS, P. (1969). *Put Away* (London: Routledge and Kegan Paul).

11. TIZARD, J., and GRAD, J. C. (1961). *The Mentally Handicapped and their Families* (London: Oxford University Press).

12. TOWNSEND, P., and WEDDERBURN, D. (1965). *The Aged and the Welfare State*. Occasional Papers of Social Administration, no. 14 (London: G. Bell & Sons Ltd).

# DISCUSSION

*In the last century Clough's lines 'Thou shalt not kill; but need'st not strive officiously to keep alive' were a slick, satirical comment. Today they describe what is often a real and agonizing choice. This modern dilemma, a recurrent theme at the meetings of the symposium, first emerged in the session on the care of severely retarded people. Despite advances in medicine, the over-all size of this group has not decreased, but its composition has changed and will probably change still further. The number of imbeciles born (with the exception of mongols) has indeed declined, but more and more are living longer and longer. The care of mentally retarded adults is as heavy a responsibility as the care of retarded children, and nowadays it is likely to be a long-term charge. As was pointed out at the first session, identification of abnormality during pregnancy and selective elimination offer the best hope of containing the problem. Clough's commandment is already relevant. At this point responsibility for decision will be shared by doctor and parents, but responsibility for the eliminations of a grossly malformed foetus at birth must lie with the obstetrician, and further crises of choice will occur at times of acute illness. How far should the doctor intervene to prolong the life of an imbecile?*

*There may be justifiable doubt about the answers to these questions, but there can be no doubt that the care of the retarded has been allowed to lag behind other medical services. Society may be at fault for not providing enough money, but administrators and doctors have erred in not ensuring that these vulnerable citizens received their fare share of admittedly scarce resources. Segregation in large isolated institutions has made it only too easy to overlook their claims. Awareness of this situation has been growing for some time, and has lately been sharpened by the Ely Report. Efforts are being made, though painfully slowly, to arrange for as many as possible of these handicapped people to rejoin the community, to provide small hostels rather than large institutions for them, to give them the chance to have some kind of a job, to split up the old monolithic hospitals into smaller units which will be associated with general hospitals. Research, treatment, and enlightened management will all be fostered by such a return to the mainstream of medicine. But even the most enthusiastic supporters of these changes admit that they will take time, and for many years we shall not be able to afford to scrap the large out-of-date institutions. It is all the more important that they should be given a fair share of money, skill, and staff if they are to make the best of a difficult job. The less isolated may prove to have a valid place in the new system, for it was suggested that, though a small unit is the best environment for small children, a larger community may have advantages for adults.*

*It is estimated that in theory somewhere between a half and a third of those now in institutions could rejoin the community. In practice this would be feasible for only a fifth. The reasons for this may be deplorable, but they exist and cannot be ignored. There is a dearth of suitable sheltered accommodation, and local authorities are dilatory in providing more. Some patients have lost touch with their families, others are irretrievably institutionalized. After-care services are inadequate. It is easier for retarded people to live in the community if they have never lost touch with it, and modern methods may improve this proportion in the future, for smaller units and intensive treatment for children, training for suitable employment, and above all more domiciliary services will all help to keep the retarded in the world of the normal. Even today about half of retarded children are living with their own families. With more and better support the number could be increased, though their new-found power of survival may later raise fresh difficulties for those who outlive their kin.*

*Despite all advances and improvements a core of the retarded will continue to need residential care, and however this is provided its success will depend on quantity and quality of staff. For those who need nursing small units attached to a general hospital would be a possible solution. Those who only need custodial care should no longer be expected to live with the physically disabled, and for them it might be possible to set up 'social health communities' as opposed to physical health communities. Perhaps, it was suggested, these might offer a twentieth-century version of the tolerant hospitality of the medieval monastery. But whatever form these communities take they would have to be staffed by what was described as people of 'strong ethics'. Another definition might be intelligent saints, and saints of any kind have never been easy to come by.*

# 5

# Policy problems in spina bifida

E. G. KNOX
MD, MRCP
*Professor of Social Medicine*
*University of Birmingham*

# Policy problems in spina bifida

In the three years 1960–2, among a total of 65,935 births in the city of Birmingham, there were 132 children with spina bifida cystica, with or without encephalocele (1). This amounts to 2·0 per 1,000 births. One hundred and four were dead by the age of 5 years and 15 of the remainder were disabled, most of them severely so. Only 13 children were alive and well and 11 of these had skin-covered lesions at birth with no paralysis. The remaining 2 had open lesions at birth, with no paralysis; they had immediate surgical closures and are now alive and well. It is evident that dramatic cures were uncommon.

It was said, after these data were published, that Birmingham had the most appalling results on record. More strictly, Birmingham had the only results on record of a full population followed for a sufficient period of time. Most epidemiological studies have concentrated upon aetiology and very few have made comprehensive appraisals of outcome. Fortunately there is now more evidence of concern and other studies are appearing (2, 3).

In the period 1960–2, treatment patterns in Birmingham were in an ambivalent state which we may refer to as 'intermediate'. That is, immediate energetic treatment was neither limited strictly to those children with prospects of a normal existence, nor was it offered systematically to all children with prospects of surviving. Indeed, immediate closure was carried out in only 5 out of 10 children with open lesions and no paralysis, but was carried out in 8 out of 54 who were paralysed. Nor was there a discernible and comprehensive pattern of co-ordination between neurosurgery, neurological and urological surveillance, urosurgery, orthopaedic surgery, family counselling, subsequent schooling provision, and other facilities. We are speaking therefore of a fairly primitive form of service, but one which is still common enough in many parts of the country.

## The clinical dilemma

Six clinical types of spina bifida can be recognized at birth. They are listed below together with the numbers of each, found in the Birmingham study.

| | |
|---|---|
| (1) Still-born or otherwise non-viable | 52 |
| (2) Skin-covered lesion, non-paralysed | 12 |
| (3) Skin-covered lesion, paralysed | 4 |
| (4) Open lesion, non-paralysed | 10 |
| (5) Open lesion, partially paralysed | 12 |
| (6) Open lesion, paraplegia | 42 |
| | 132 |

Classes 1, 2, and 3 *never* require treatment within 48 hours. Class 4 *always* requires treatment within 48 hours. Classes 5 and 6 contain the immediate clinical dilemma. It appears that for class 6, primary closure within 48 hours and suitable later treatment for hydrocephalus and urinary obstruction in particular, will result in the survival of about 50 per cent, but they will be paralysed to a greater or lesser degree, and mostly severely. Non-energetic treatment on the other hand will still result in the survival of 5–10 per cent, also paralysed.

In class 5, much the same applies, but with the additional possibility that early intervention may in some cases reduce the severity of the subsequent paralysis. However, this is a relatively small group and in practice most of these children are severely disabled. Therefore the essential decision is whether early intervention should be limited to class 4, or whether provision should be made to extend it to all viable children with open lesions. There is little to support the validity of a selective intervention policy for these two classes based on degrees of paralyses as ascertained within the few hours available for the clinical decision. There may, however, by a basis for selection according to the degree of hydrocephalus present at birth.

A selective policy based on parental attitudes and values is scarcely possible for the majority of cases, and where the parents' views can be taken into account this would usually take the form of modifying a background policy.

In terms of the development of a clinical policy the situation appears to be bi-stable and 'intermediate' levels of practice can be envisaged only as an interim position.

## The need for a policy

Policy considerations arise at at least three levels.

### AT A CLINICAL LEVEL

The urgency of the decision requirements when an affected child is encountered are such that the clinician usually has a need for a previously thought-out attitude, although not necessarily a fixed one. The terms of the two main alternative policies have been laid out above.

### AT THE LEVEL OF DEPLOYING EXISTING RESOURCES

If existing resources are to be organized so that they are deployed effectively, a formulation of policy is needed. Whether the policy chosen be a universally activist approach, or a selectively activist approach, it may serve as a basis for co-ordinating neurosurgical, urosurgical, orthopaedic, paediatric, and other services to the benefit of affected children. However, if the policy choice is seen as one between an activist policy and no policy at all, then it is unlikely that anything but the first will bring effective care to bear on those to whom it is allocated.

### AT THE LEVEL OF DEPLOYING NEW RESOURCES

New resources are awarded competitively in the face of conflicting assessments of priority, coming from different quarters. There is no stereotype for the nature of the competition. In one case, limited finance or limited premises or limited nursing staff might have to be allocated either to a neonatal neurological surgery or to neonatal cardiac surgery. At another level the competition for resources may be between hospital expansion, or the expansion of community screening services. However, there cannot even be an application for resources unless a policy has been defined and, usually, unless that policy is backed by at least a projection of anticipated benefits.

## The question of consistency

We see that there is a strong argument for a policy of some kind but a serious difficulty as to what that policy should be. The situation with spina bifida is such that the decision cannot be a private one. Yet a firm consensus probably could not be obtained between different clinicians, and between different areas, and between different levels, as outlined. Differences between clinicians within particular administrative areas are probably the basis of the frequent lack of policy at the administrative levels. Differences between administrative areas are probably of less importance, and provided that they have positive policies it is probable that any policy is better than none. Differences between administrative levels result in uncomfortable confrontations and (this is quite a general matter, not limited to the problem of spina bifida) the clinicians may come to one conclusion and the administrators to another. Orthodox wisdom suggests that both parties may be right within their appropriate frames of references. The clinician is right to press for facilities and meanwhile do the best he can with what he has. The administrator is right to divert his limited resources to competitively favourable areas but leave the clinician to deploy what he has, as he thinks fit.

It cannot be denied, however, that resolution of the problem in these terms is uncomfortable and invites a consideration of both the administrative logic and the administrative justice involved. Is it in fact *logical* that two bodies can come correctly to opposed conclusions? And is it *fair* that a clinician is left with the responsibility to decide upon a policy but be denied the resources to implement it? One is reminded sympathetically of the doctor in charge of a dialysis unit who sent the waiting-list to the HMC to decide who should die.

### ADMINISTRATIVE LOGIC

The trouble with logic is that we expect it to be universally applicable. If we think of a hierarchical administrative decision tree as analogous with a computer program comprising subroutines within subroutines, then we expect a certain consistency between the parts. However, the logic of computer programs works on decisions about the similarity between or the difference between essentially numerical values. The analogy between numerical comparisons and qualitative preferences is tempting but misleading. It is possible to construct preference-scoring systems which compare pairs of choices (diagnoses, candidates, policy formulations, washing machines, distinction awards, motor-cars, . . ., etc.) such that *A* is preferred to *B*, *B* is preferred to *C*, *C* is preferred to *D*, yet *D* is preferred to *A*. Our intuitive reluctance to believe in a circular order of merit arises from a temptation to believe that the relationship 'is preferred to' is exactly equivalent to the relationship 'is greater than'. Unfortunately, 'is greater than' is a transitive relationship so that if *A* is greater than *B* and *B* is greater than *C* then *A* must be greater than *C*; but preference relationships are not transitive and this is why circular preference orders can result (4, 5). When the matter is complicated by a hierarchical decision-structure with different frames of reference at each level, anything can happen. There is little doubt that inconsistent conclusions can coexist without contradiction and we would deceive ourselves if we thought we could solve this kind of problem simply by attention to logic.

ADMINISTRATIVE JUSTICE

The most obvious injustices arise when the methods of distributing the resources and the methods of distributing the responsibilities are inconsistent with each other. A familiar example in the university world (with respect to the UGC in particular) is where application for resources is required on an earmarked basis, but where the block allocation of resources is provided on a non-earmarked basis and is usually less than is asked for. The applicant is left with the responsibility but without the means. Conversely, if an application is made on a total evaluation of needs but the resources are accompanied by detailed direction on deployment, then the applicant may be left without resources to carry out his other commitments. It should generally be assumed that hierarchically superior and inferior bodies *will* disagree on deployment if they get the chance and that the best that can be hoped for is that they should agree what kinds of decision belong to each and that the appropriate resources should be allocated with the responsibility.

However, this is a council of perfection and in practice neither medical needs nor responsibilities are amenable to a comprehensive and semantically clear classification. 'Is it fair?' is perhaps a better question to ask of an administrative impasse than 'Is it logical?', but we could be equally misled if we relied upon it.

## Perpetual confrontation

If we can find definitive solutions to policy confrontations neither on the basis of logic nor justice, and it appears that a search for consistency is likely to be disappointed, what should be our aims? If a consistent policy cannot be imposed, perhaps the best we can do is to engineer a situation in which it might develop. Our aim should not be the complete avoidance of abrasive relationships but only the avoidance of fruitless ones and the engineering of constructive confrontations. The most promising environment for this is probably a factual one and our best short-term aim is the design of a monitoring system which records and makes available in particular areas a running statement of the occurrence of the disease, of the treatments supplied and not supplied, and of the outcomes in terms of survival, the effects on families, and the load of treatment and the quality of life of the survivors.

### REFERENCES

1. KNOX, E. G. (1967). 'Spina bifida in Birmingham', *Dev. med. child. neurol.* **9**, 645–6.
2. LAURENCE, K. M. Chapter 6 in this volume.
3. SPAIN, BERNADETTE (1970). *Quarterly Bulletin of Research of the Intelligence Unit of the Greater London Council*, no. 12.
4. GARDNER, M. (1970). 'The paradox of the nontransitive dice and the elusive principle of indifference', *Scient. Am.* **223**, no. 6, 110.
5. Peripatetic correspondence (1971). *Lancet*, **i**, 232.

# 6

# The changing problem of spina bifida

K. M. LAURENCE
MA, MB, FRCPath
*Department of Child Health*
*Welsh National School of Medicine*
*Cardiff*

# The changing problem of spina bifida

## Introduction

Anencephaly, encephalocele, spina bifida cystica (myelocele, myelomeningocele, and meningocele), and certain forms of spina bifida occulta are all part of a family of conditions inter-related aetiologically and are all different end-products of the same general process, namely failure of the neural tube to close properly in the first four weeks after conception. The evidence for this is both clinical in that any of these may be found associated in the same family (1), and experimental, as any condition may be produced in an experimental animal by the use of a wide variety of teratogenic influences, such as drugs, deficiencies, X-rays, and dyes, provided they are given in the right dose and during the teratogenic period of pregnancy (2).

Spina bifida cystica and encephalocele has an incidence in the British Isles varying from over 4 per 1,000 births in South Wales to less than 1·5 per 1,000 births in East Anglia, with the national average of about 2·5 per 1,000 births. The 2,600 cases born each year in these islands include about 130 cases of meningocele who should be normal both physically and mentally, and 170 encephaloceles most of whom tend to be severely retarded though physically they may not be markedly affected. The remaining cases consist of various forms of myelocele, most of whom have an open lesion liable to infection and who, directly as a result of the spinal cord malformation suffer from varying degrees of physical handicap in the form of lower limb muscle and sphincter paralysis. They are none the less potentially at least relatively un-affected mentally.

However, the majority have some hydrocephalus when born which is often progressive but may arrest spontaneously. The degree of hydrocephalus to some extent determines the mental ability with the more severely hydrocephalic having a poorer performance both intellectually and neurologically (4). Ascending infection, especially if it fails to respond rapidly to therapy also leads to brain damage, sometimes with dire effect on ability. Indeed, this is the immediate cause of deficit in the worst affected cases.

## Outcome without surgery

To get a 'baseline' against which to judge the results of surgery the problem was investigated by looking at the survival in children born at a time when only general nursing care, and possibly antibiotic cover was given. All the cases born in South Wales in a community of 850,000, over a seven-year period (1956–62 inclusive) with 102,000 births, were ascertained. A total of 425 cases was found, giving an incidence of 4·13 cases of spina bifida cystica and encephalocele per 1,000 total births (6). One-quarter of these are still-born, often with gross hydrocephalus or other serious associated and unrelated abnormalities. Of the 315 live-born, 24 died during the first day and 32 more succumbed by the end of the first week, a total of 17 per cent, due to the usual perinatal causes or the grossness of the malformation or associated lesions. A further 56 per cent of these live births died during the next nine months of the complications of spina bifida, the usual cause of death being meningitis or hydrocephalus. Only a further 20 cases (7 per cent of the live births) died after that time, one of the commoner causes of death being renal failure often consequent upon pyeloniephritis (Figure 6.1). Sixty-three cases (20 per cent of the live births) survived including all the 18 meningoceles born during this time, 8 of the 26 encephaloceles, and 37 of the 274 myeloceles. Nearly all the meningoceles were physically normal, or near normal, and they had a mean IQ of 94 (Table 6.1 and Figure 6.2). Half of the encephaloceles were physically normal, the remainder very grossly handicapped and all were well below average mentally, the mean IQ being 56. Although the myeloceles contained a disproportionate number of milder cases, as a group, physically they fared little better with only one-third having little

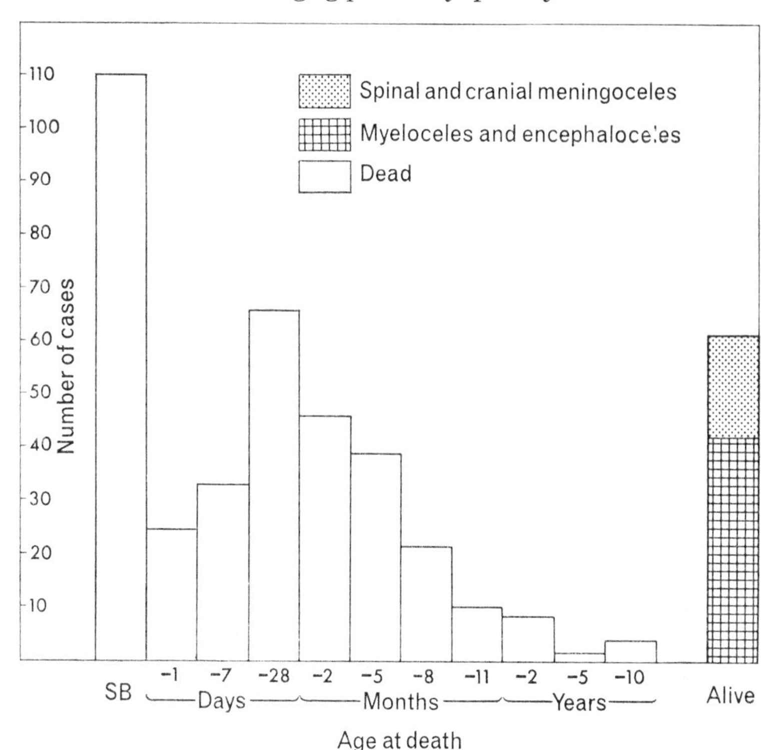


**Figure 6.1.** The survival of 425 cases of spina bifida cystica and cranium bifidium cysticum (reprinted by permission of the Editor of *Archives of Disease in Childhood*, from the paper by Laurence and Tew (6)).

or no obvious physical disability and the great majority being severely handicapped with leg paralysis or incontinence or both. Intellectually, they showed quite a wide spread of ability (mean IQ 90) with a fair number of average and some superior individuals. A number were grossly retarded, usually those who had had repeated attacks of meningitis in infancy, or who developed severe hydrocephalus. One wonders whether the handicap, both physical and mental, of some of these survivors might not have been less had these individuals had the benefit of more active and effective treatment.

In the absence of active modern treatment, therefore, only few children survive and, many of those who do are either relatively mild cases requiring little supportive treatment and probably no

**Table 6.1.** *Physical disabilities in sixty-three survivors* (6).

| *Degree of handicap* | *Examples of disabilities* | Number of cases *Meningocele* | *Myelocele* | *Encephalocele* |
|---|---|---|---|---|
| Normal | None | 13 | 2 | 4 |
| Minimal | Physical deformity only<br>Squint<br>Slight imbalance<br>Slight limp | 3 | 7 | — |
| Moderate | Partial paralysis but walking without aids<br>Enuresis | — | 2 | — |
| Severe | Walking with aids only (partial paralysis)<br>Partial incontinence only<br>Severe imbalance<br>Incontinence with successful diversion<br>Partial blindness | 2 | 10 | 1 |
| Very severe | Complete incontinence (untreated)<br>Wheelchair existence (complete paralysis)<br>Blindness | — | 15 | 1 |
| Incapacitating | Vegetative existence | — | 1 | 2 |
| | TOTAL | 18 | 37 | 8 |

special educational facilities, or very grossly handicapped, many of whom, in the past at least, would have been institutionalized. Thus in the past this problem therefore did not obtrude itself too much on the consciousness either of the profession or the general public.

## Outcome with modern surgery

The current active approach to this problem consists of immediate closure of the open lesion, the prompt drainage of progressive hydrocephalus and vigorous exhibition of antibiotics for intracranial and renal infection, and urinary diversion, if necessary. By effectively closing the open spinal lesion not only is infection excluded, thus avoiding one of the major causes of brain damage, but also an unsightly tumour removed which may later present big nursing problems. Effective methods of dealing with progressive hydrocephalus such as the Holter ventriculo-atrial shunt operation have now been available for fifteen years, thus enabling the other major cause of mental retardation to be minimized.

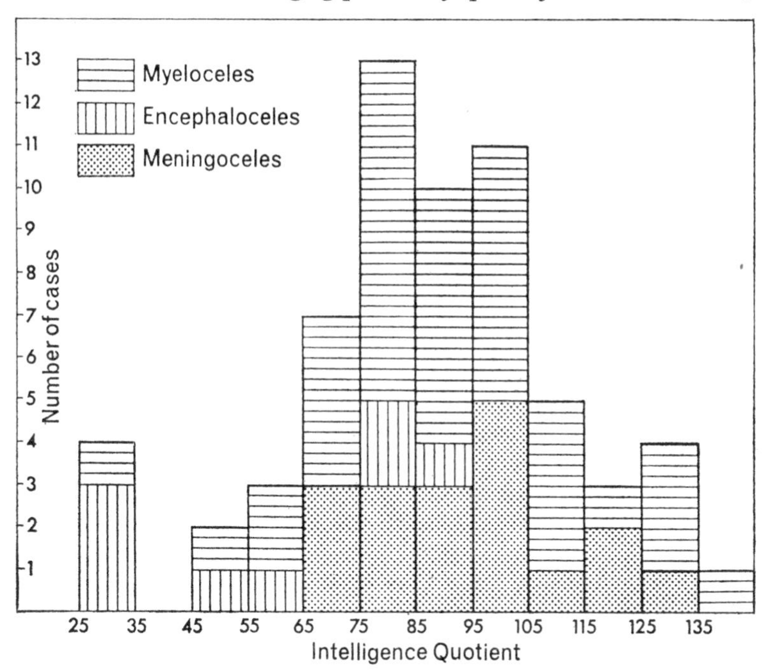


**Figure 6.2.** A histogram of the Intelligence Quotient results on 63 survivors with spina bifida cystica and cranium bifidium cysticum (reprinted by permission of the Editor of *Archives of Disease in Childhood*, from the paper by Laurence and Tew (6)).

Modern antibiotics and the urinary diversion procedures carried out during the second or third year of life will help to achieve continence and help to avoid renal damage, one of the major causes of death in older children.

Even with the most active therapy nothing could probably be done for the 17 per cent who die of perinatal causes, but the additional 63 per cent who die thereafter do so largely as a result of preventable causes and therefore by active effective intervention at least 80 per cent of those born alive with this group of deformities should be potentially salvageable. It is for this 80 per cent of the live-borns in the community that any surgical and other services have to be planned. Indeed, this goal is being approached in a number of centres such as Liverpool, where the survival in the cases operated upon between 1960 and 1962 is over twice that in the South Wales unoperated series (8), and has been rising to

70 per cent in cases dealt with more recently (7). In South Wales, too, the survival to school age in cases born between 1964 and 1965 has increased to 50 per cent. Undoubtedly, by these methods some of the brain damage, paralysis, and incontinence seen in the untreated survivors is being avoided, but at the same time more very severely deformed and handicapped children are being enabled to survive.

## Load on medical services

The intensive care and the increased survival is now placing considerable strain on the medical services, for these children have to attend hospital at frequent intervals to enable a careful watch to be kept on the hydrocephalus for the valve operations are not without their complications of blockage and infection when revision may be necessary at short notice. The urinary tract has to be kept under constant surveillance for infection which may be insidious and devastating in its effects. There may well have to be frequent attendances and an admission for orthopaedic manipulation and operations to help with ambulation, and with appliance fitting. The load is thus considerable and of course accumulative. In South Wales, for example, some fifty long-term survivors are now being added to existing numbers each succeeding year. With the improvement in techniques this annual addition could well increase over the years.

## Strain on the family

The burden upon the family unit can also be considerable. This is being investigated in a longitudinal study being carried out in South Wales (3). In this study the parents were first interviewed within a few days of the birth of the malformed child and at regular intervals thereafter. The oldest of the children concerned in this study are now approaching their seventh birthdays. It was found that the way parents were told of the malformation in the first instance varied considerably and their reaction varied likewise with fathers often being more distressed than the mothers. On the whole it was carried out reasonably sympathetically but some parents seem to have had justifiable criticisms. The reaction of the relatives and neighbours tended to be helpful and supportive. Thoughtless remarks seemed rare. On the other hand one-third of fathers and more than half of the mothers felt that they could have been given more advice and support and sympathy by their hospital consultants, their GPs, or their health visitors. Some parents felt that they should have been told more about what is being done and what is being planned to be done and why. The emotional and physical strain of having and caring for a malformed child might have been thought to adversely influence marital harmony. In the great majority of families however, whether the child survived or not the parents said that the event had brought them closer together. While the child was young there was only one instance where it had precipitated family break-up. However, as the problems multiply and the parents are unable to escape the realities that their child is severely handicapped or possibly retarded, marital problems seem to multiply. Crisis points seem to arise about the age of 2 years and about the time when the child enters school.

Local social work support, sometimes financial support or help with special equipment or appliances, the provision of a conveniently sited home, or the alteration of an existing one to ease the problem of caring for a handicapped child seem obvious enough, but may be difficult to obtain in practice. The need for a holiday is now increasingly recognized and patients may be admitted to hospital temporarily to enable the family to get away, or special holiday facilities are provided where the holiday can be taken with the affected child.

The occurrence of a malformation inevitably colours the parents' attitude towards having further children. Many parents know vaguely that there is a recurrence risk and a few seek expert genetic advice. An appreciable proportion of the latter decide to limit the family, especially if they have already got one or more normal children, or if the spina bifida child is surviving. The normal brothers and sisters of spina bifida children especially if severely handicapped, often show degrees of maladjustment, probably because of the disproportionate parental time and energy that may be devoted to the handicapped sib.

## Schooling and employment

It appears that to begin with at least about half the children, though sometimes severely handicapped both physically and perhaps mentally are accommodated in normal nursery and infant schools. Some, however, have to go to special schooling or training facilities or if these are not readily to hand be given home tuition. A number are so grossly handicapped that they are not capable of benefiting from schooling at all and are merely receiving nursing care at home or are institutionalized. It is likely that as these children get older increasing difficulties will arise with the more handicapped individuals in normal schools, and they will have to be found places in the special schools which in many instances are already under pressure.

In one large school for 135 physically handicapped children in South Wales, between 1958 and 1963 less than 8 per cent of the admissions to the school were of children with spina bifida cystica. Between 1964 and 1966 this figure rose to 21 per cent and since 1967 it has risen to over 34 per cent. The proportion of the admissions with this condition is likely to rise further for in the current year spina bifida has accounted for half the new pupils taken in.

The problem of finding employment for these individuals when they leave school is now being given some thought. It is likely that few at all severely handicapped with this group of malformations will be able to be employed in the 'open' and many will have to be offered 'sheltered jobs' if indeed they are able to gainfully work at all. The others will have to be 'occupied' in as satisfying a manner as possible.

## Selection for surgery

With the mounting strain on medical services alone a measure of selection for surgery will certainly be called for increasingly. Unfortunately immediately after birth it is almost impossible to predict the eventual outcome of a case. Although most of the mildly affected cases tend to survive with less handicap this is by no means invariable. Nor is it certain that all the severely paralysed infants with gross lesions will die. Few will deny the optimum treatment for the former but the latter present more of a problem. It is probably quite justifiable to exclude certain new-born from any surgical procedures who have either a very poor prognosis for survival or for a survival with a reasonable intellect. For example, infants with severe hydrocephalus at birth who have little prospect of surviving with even low normal intellect, those with severe resistant meningitis or ventriculitis who will almost certainly have severe brain damage, those with a high kyphosis which tends to become progressively worse and lead to gross crippling and sooner or later to respiratory death, those with established renal failure without infection at birth, and those with other severe unassociated malformations, should probably not be operated upon. Selection of less severely affected infants at or about the time of birth is a very much more difficult matter in view of the problem of prognostication. However, an attempt is at this time being made to devise a selection procedure on the basis of the degree of hydrocephalus, or paralysis, and of incontinence. In some others who have survived, sometimes after perhaps a number of interventions, a point must inevitably come when further therapeutic efforts may not be warranted in a particular individual who may not be capable of a reasonable life because of severe mental retardation or very gross crippling in limb or renal tract. It must be remembered that each intervention adds trauma both mental and physical to the child and his parents and each individual intervention may divert therapeutic efforts from other possibly more rewarding cases. The decision in the neonatal period must be a medical one. Not only can parents rarely be in possession of all the facts quickly enough to make a decision in an 'emergency' situation, but also they are usually not in a fit emotional state for a reasoned judgement. Also they should not be left with the possibility of carrying the guilt that a refusal to give permission to operate might entail. The decision later on not to persist with treatment in an obviously hopeless case should probably also be largely a professional one, but now the parents must inevitably play a greater part. Indeed the initiative at times comes first from them.

## Conclusion

Spina bifida, with its burden for the family, the increasing problems for the medical services, the social, the educational, and eventually the employment services thus presents a very special and poignant situation. One is dealing with the problems of a child who may be very severely handicapped physically, who is relatively intact mentally and who has insight into his predicament.

He cannot be abandoned if in the struggle to preserve life, with all its trauma, something more than just survival is salvageable.

## Summary

With the national incidence of spina bifida cystica and encephalocele of about 2·5 per 1,000 births some 2,600 cases are born each year in the UK. One in 20 of these is a meningocele, a less serious condition, 1 in 15 is an encephalocele, usually a closed but serious lesion, and the remainder are myeloceles, mostly open and often associated with hydrocephalus and limb and sphincter paralysis.

One-quarter of the myeloceles and encephaloceles are still-born and if left untreated most of the remainder will die; 17 per cent succumb in the first week of perinatal causes, 56 per cent during the next nine months, largely of hydrocephalus or meningitis, and 7 per cent after that time generally of renal failure. Twenty per cent survive including many of the encephaloceles, mostly grossly retarded and all the meningoceles who tend to be near normal. The surviving myeloceles who include a relatively large number of less severely affected are none the less mostly physically handicapped but relatively intact mentally.

Modern therapy in the form of antibiotics, immediate closure of the open lesion, and the effective treatment of hydrocephalus is enabling a large proportion (80 per cent) who survive the first week to live. Indeed additional spinal cord damage from infection and brain damage from infection and progressive hydrocephalus undoubtedly seen in some untreated cases is avoided, but many of these survivors are very severely paralysed and malformed, and will require repeated, prolonged, and complicated orthopaedic surgery to improve posture and ambulation, and urological surgery to prevent renal infection and failure and achieve continence. Some of those that survive to school age will require special schooling or even just custodial care and one does not know yet how many will eventually be able to hold down a job and lead a 'normal' life.

A few parents do not come to terms with the malformation from the start, occasionally because of mishandling of the situation immediately after birth, but outright rejection is rare. Parents often find the constant visiting while their children are in hospital and the repeated out-patient attendances a severe mental, physical, and financial burden but it is generally cheerfully borne, sometimes to the detriment of personal health, family welfare, and sometimes the marriage itself. The fear of a recurrence in a subsequent pregnancy will frequently limit the family especially when the survivor requires constant attention. Hospital and other staffs sometimes do not lighten the burden through lack of communication and explanation.

All this places a tremendous burden on the patient himself, the parents and the medical, social, and education and other services. A point must come when further therapeutic efforts are not warranted in a particular individual, bearing in mind the eventual result and the trauma both mental and physical that each further intervention inflicts upon all those immediately involved and the inevitable effect each would have on diverting resources from other individuals who might benefit more.

## REFERENCES


1. Carter, C. O., Laurence, K. M., and David, P. A. (1968). 'A family study of major central nervous system malformations in South Wales', *J. med. Genet.* **5,** 81.
2. Giroud, A. (1960). 'Causes and morphogenesis of anencephaly', in Wolstenholme, G. E. W., and O'Connor, C. M. (eds), *Ciba Foundation Symposium on Congenital Malformations*, p. 199 (London: J. & A. Churchill).
3. Hare, E. H., Laurence, K. M., Payne, H., and Rawnsley, K. (1966). 'Spina bifida cystica and family stress', *Br. med. J.* **2,** 757–60.
4. Laurence, K. M. (1969). 'Neurological and intellectual sequelae of hydrocephalus', *Arch. Neurol.* **20,** 73.
5. —— Carter, C. O., and David, P. A. (1968). 'The major central nervous system malformations in South Wales. I. Incidence, local variations and geographic factors', *Br. J. prev. soc. Med.* **22,** 146.
6. —— and Tew, B. J. (1971). 'Natural history of spina bifida cystica and cranium bifidum cysticum. Major central nervous system malformations in South Wales, Part IV', *Archives of Disease in Childhood,* **46,** 127–38.
7. Mawdsley, T., and Rickham, P. P. (1969). 'Further follow-up study of early operation for open myelomeningocele', *Develop. med. Child Neurol.* **11,** suppl. 20, 8.
8. Rickham, P. P., and Mawdsley, T. (1966). 'The effect of early operation on the survival of spina bifida cystica', ibid. **8**, suppl. 11, 20.

# DISCUSSION

*Quality of survival, deployment of resources, and responsibility for decision-taking were again the main themes of the discussion on children with spina bifida. But the group presents some special problems. Though their number is small, these children are usually very disabled both physically and sometimes mentally, and they will require not only continued support but also continued surgery. The decision to take the first step towards their precarious survival must be taken within twenty-four hours of birth, and it must therefore be made by the obstetrician. A later decison, whether to continue with surgery, may lie with the parents who, with medical counsel, should have the right to say enough is enough. But the first decision must be the obstetrician's, and the increasing number of survivals is probably partly due to a change in obstetric practice. Advances in neonatal and paediatric surgery today give the child a chance of survival which the obstetrician is reluctant to deny it. His traditional role as a selector for survival has been sharply curtailed. Yet once the first step is taken, responsibility for the child's care lies not with decision-making obstetricians, but with his surgical and paediatric colleagues, the child's family, and the social and educational services.*

*For a small number of infants the choice is easy. A few are clearly too malformed ever to achieve a tolerable existence. A few others are clearly viable projects, but for the larger group of in-between, difficult individual decisions must be made. At present it is impossible to codify criteria, for the after-life of the children already saved by operation lies in the still unknown future. But already some special schools are at breaking-point and find it difficult to cope with 'the stacking-up of helpless little creatures'. When some of these 'rescued' children reach the stage of secondary education there is likely to be an even greater crisis.*

*The deployment of resources it was suggested, could be settled at national, regional, or hospital level, but the decision on each child at any rate in the first instance, must rest with the doctor, and he must be left free to act as he thinks best. More adequate information about resources and long-term prognosis will help him, and we have now reached a stage when we are beginning to realize what can be done, and what quality of survival can be achieved. But on-going monitoring is badly needed, and it would still be foolhardy to attempt to formulate rigid criteria and unwise and unkind to publicize them.*

# 7

# Intensive care and its limits, particularly in keeping alive the very ill

G. T. SPENCER
FFA, RCS
*Consultant in charge of the Intensive Therapy Unit*
*St Thomas's Hospital*

# Intensive care and its limits, particularly in keeping alive the very ill

THE principles and aims of intensive care have been described in the first report of the BMA Planning Unit (1). Intensive care is not a new medical specialty nor an extension to such specialties as anaesthesia, clinical physiology, or pharmacology. It is simply a method of organizing medical and nursing care so that expertise and equipment can be concentrated where they are most needed. Thus a major contribution of the intensive care unit is to make the most efficient use of severely limited skilled staff and thus provide an acceptable standard of care for patients whose needs are greatest.

With increasing medical specialization the larger hospitals have spawned a great variety of special function units, each devoted to the investigation and treatment of a particular medical problem. This system permits valuable clinical investigation and satisfies the professional desire for empire-building. All medical staff have the same interest; this reduces conflict and allows leadership to be based on status alone. If a patient fails to fit into the appropriate diagnostic category or develops multisystem disease, he may be in trouble. This problem is not new. Surgeons have for years claimed, with occasional justification, that the most dangerous place in which to perforate a peptic ulcer is in a medical ward. But with divisions, specialties, and super specialties the danger can only be accentuated.

The essential differences between a special function unit and an intensive care unit should be that the medical staffing of an intensive care unit is multidiscipline, the unit is centralized and functions as a service department.

If the doctors can only be persuaded, even for short periods, to live together amicably the benefits to the care of the critically ill can be startling. The high staff/patient ratio makes complicated therapy easy to perform. The range of medical expertise constantly present can be wide, thus minimizing errors of omission and lessening errors of commission due to intemperate individual enthusiasm. The medical problems of the critically ill are rarely limited to one system and a team approach to therapy is the only satisfactory method.

The best way of organizing and establishing such a unit is bound to vary from one hospital to another, depending on its workload and staff structure. Some clinicians tended initially to view intensive care with suspicion, feeling that it might disrupt continuity of clinical management. Experience suggests that where units have been successfully established this suspicion is quickly dispelled as the advantages so clearly outweigh the undoubted disadvantages and difficulties.

Despite the now considerable experience of intensive care units, convincing evidence of their value is difficult to obtain. The techniques of controlled trial can rarely be applied and the reports of case series from intensive care units are difficult to evaluate due to diversity of clinical material. Once such services are available most clinicians regard it as unethical to withhold them arbitrarily in order to measure their benefits. In a limited sense, this fact is in itself a justification. The selection of patients for admission is somewhat capricious. Attempts to establish medical criteria for admission have rarely been successful and requests for admission are commonly related to deficiencies in twenty-four-hour cover elsewhere in the hospital. All this merely emphasizes the difficulty of establishing the medical value of intensive care. It does not release us from the obligation of attempting to do so, particularly as the high cost of intensive care has to be considered in relation to other medical needs.

My own experience over five years in a 10-bed teaching hospital unit suggests that the current cost per bed per week is approximately £450, about 80 per cent of this is due to salaries and is therefore roughly constant whether the unit is full or empty. Thus the total cost of the unit is £4,500 per week or £234,000 per annum. About 500 patients per annum pass through and the mortality in the unit remains constant between 19 and 21 per cent, although the workload has changed considerably over the years. Of the 80 per cent who leave the unit alive, a further 5 per cent die subsequently without leaving hospital. Thus about 375 patients per annum survive to leave hospital and the essential question is what proportion of these would have died without our expensive efforts. Viewing our figures as pessimistically as possible I have concluded that in no more than 10 per cent can one say with certainty that the unit has saved life which would have been lost without it. That is 50 lives per year or £4,680 per life. These figures are obviously crude in the extreme. They take no account of the quality of survival which ranges from normal to severely limited. Nor do they allow for the considerable research, development, and teaching benefits accruing from the unit, some of which would certainly not occur without it.

Fundamentally valuable information rarely accrues from clinical research on the critically ill, and it is only ethically acceptable if it offers potential therapeutic benefit to the individual subject. Nevertheless, many people spend their working lives elucidating the precise function of the dying myocardium and developing therapeutic techniques for minimizing by a barely detectable margin the effects of this inexorable process. Money for such studies is readily forthcoming due to the emotional impact of the terminal stages in a mortal disease. A serious disadvantage of intensive care is that it tends to concentrate research money and effort on end stage disease. Basic research into the causes of atherosclerosis, though less dramatic in its appeal, is probably in the longer term more productive. Thus the research benefit from intensive care is limited. As the idea of intensive care first arose from the need to segregate patients receiving complicated treatment involving mechanical or electrical apparatus, it is hardly surprising that its greatest contribution continues to be the practical development and trial of new techniques. The benefit here is considerable. A new method always seems complicated and often is. As it becomes established it gets easier, simpler, and safer, and can be used more widely. Fifteen years ago artificial respiration by intermittent positive pressure via a tracheotomy was exciting and complicated. The mortality directly attributable to the method was 30–40 per cent. Today it is routine; the residual mortality, due to carelessness and human error, is tiny and significant numbers of patients permanently on respirators live worthwhile lives at home. Some even develop an earning capacity and become financially self-supporting. We now maintain 42 such patients, who have lived at home receiving continuous artificial respiration via tracheotomies for periods of up to nine years. Their combined experience at home totals 246 years. In the past five years two have died from preventable technical disasters. I have accompanied two on continental holidays and taken one in a cable car to a height of 9,000 feet in the Alps. They call themselves 'responauts' and have formed a club which maintains an active magazine to which they contribute articles and pool experience, difficulties, and needs. The commonest disease from which they suffer is, of course, respiratory poliomyelitis, of which there have been five new cases in young adults in south-east England this year. Others include sufferers from high cervical cord trauma, myasthenia gravis, kyphoscoliosis, motor neurone disease, chronic polyneuritis (Guillian Barrie syndrome), and chronic bronchitis.

Efficient artificial ventilation of the lungs is without doubt the greatest single therapeutic advance which has resulted from intensive care. Apart from the almost bizarre achievements of some patients who remain permanently dependent on artifiicial respiration, its application as an acute therapeutic measure has revolutionized the management of many diseases, for example, tetanus, drug overdosage, severe status asthmaticus, and status epilepticus. Its use is routine following cardiac surgery and chest injuries, and the current problem is no longer when and how to use it but how to decide when its use is unjustifiable or should be discontinued.

The greatest gain from intensive care is in the management of unconscious patients, the management of patients following cardiac surgery, and the management of patients with respiratory failure from almost any cause. In the first and third group particularly, efficient intensive care can prolong life almost indefinitely. The consequences of eliminating these common modes of death are profound and are only beginning to be appreciated. The bulk of neurosurgical experience in this country is accrued in specialist neurological and neurosurgical hospitals where respiratory care, being secondary to the hospital's main function, is commonly secondary in quality. Paradoxically, this may be a good thing. Provided respiratory care is adequate to maintain life while acute neurological investigation and treatment is undertaken, this is sufficient. The second and third weeks of artificial ventilation and tracheotomy care are the most hazardous, and if neurological recovery has not by then started the patient usually succumbs without excessive and useless prolongation of a semi-vegetable existence. Top-quality respiratory care may prevent this merciful release. A highly trained nursing and physiotherapeutic team cannot be instructed to use less than their normal skill. If cerebral damage is gross and amounts to complete destruction this is usually apparent. Suitable measures can be taken and useful donor organs for transplantation may be obtained. If cerebral damage is relatively slight, recovery occurs without the need for expert respiratory care. Unfortunately many patients fall between the two grades. Over the past five years my own unit has produced 37 permanent imbeciles. Even with the wisdom of hindsight it is hard to say that in any of them life was officiously maintained when it need not have been. In every case competent neurological or neurosurgical opinion was obtained and the advice given was that the chances of survival justified continuance of intensive care. I hope that with more experience our imbecile production rate will decline, but at present it is still higher than their death-rate. It seems clear that until neurological assessment improves, intensive care is not an unmixed blessing. Facilities for the long-term care of these unfortunate victims of sophisticated medicine are even more inadequate than geriatric facilities. Few families can cope with such a person at home, and even if they can, the effects on the rest of the family are unacceptable. The satisfaction of glittering successes does not entirely compensate for these disasters.

Although these people usually recover sufficiently to be transferred to general hospital wards, the same does not always apply to patients who remain partly or completely dependent on respiratory aids following intensive care. Many units have found their disposal to be a problem. Their equipment and its efficient use at all times makes them unsuitable for the general ward with its rapidly changing staff of student nurses, many of whom will never have seen or used such equipment before. In an attempt to solve this problem we were persuaded three years ago to take over an old poliomyelitis unit in an equally old fever hospital. With suitable injections of cash and the exchange of staff from the main unit who needed a rest from the rigours of acute intensive care, a unit has been established which is attempting to rehabilitate these patients and teach them and their families to live with their disability. The problems are not dissimilar to those of home-based chronic dialysis and the organization is much the same. Although our experience is limited at present, the prospects look hopeful and the greatest enthusiasm comes from the patients themselves, whose determination to survive and surmount their disabilities is prodigious.

## Conclusions

Intensive care is undoubtedly a valuable and constructive therapeutic method which saves lives. It nevertheless creates as many problems as it solves and can distort medical priorities.

At present, therefore, our aim should probably not be to make sophisticated intensive care universally available. It is better confined to centres of medical research and teaching. Part of that teaching must always be to detect situations and patients for whom intensive care is not justifiable or desirable and to recognize that the aim of medicine is not to prolong life at any cost.

## Summary

The principles and aims of intensive care have been described in the first report of the BMA Planning Unit (1).

In district general hospitals the value of an intensive care unit is primarily to concentrate severely limited skilled staff into one or more areas in order to provide an acceptable standard of care for patients whose needs are greatest.

In teaching centres, where staff tend to be more plentiful, intensive care units make possible techniques of investigation and therapy which are impossible in general wards. A brief outline of the organization and cost of such a unit is given and an attempt made to show how it has developed over the past five years and may continue to develop in the future.

The value of such a unit is difficult to assess. The normal techniques of controlled trial cannot be applied. Once such services are available, most clinicians regard it as unethical to withhold them arbitrarily in order to measure their benefits. In a limited sense, this fact is a justification for such units.

The selection of patients for admission is capricious. Attempts to establish medical criteria for admission have rarely been successful. The routine prophylactic use of low-grade intensive care, for example in myocardial infarction, has yet to prove its value, and requests for admission are commonly related to deficiencies in twenty-four-hour cover elsewhere in the hospital.

The greatest gain from intensive care is in the management of unconscious patients, the management of patients following cardiac surgery, and the management of patients with respiratory failure from any cause. In the first and third groups particularly, efficient intensive care can prolong life almost indefinitely. The consequences of eliminating these common modes of death are profound and are only beginning to be appreciated. Facilities for the long-term care of such survivors are even more inadequate than geriatric facilities. A brief description of a long-term respiratory rehabilitation project established in an attempt to solve one aspect of this problem is given.

## REFERENCE

1. BRITISH MEDICAL ASSOCIATION (1967). *Intensive Care.* BMA Planning Unit Report no. 1 (London: British Medical Association).

# DISCUSSION

*Intensive care units are expensive to run and greedy for staff and equipment. Dr Spencer's honest perplexity as to how much is actually gained from them stimulated a wide-ranging discussion on the techniques and purposes of cost-analysis and its application to medicine. Though administrators and laymen who have the responsibility for allocating resources and grants badly need facts to guide them, these are difficult to collect and often of doubtful value when collected, partly because of the difficulty of maintaining adequate yet humane control groups and partly because so many imponderables intrude into any medical study.*

*Statistical inquiries can be more appropriately used in prophylactic than curative medicine. Bradford Hill, for instance, was able to devise an acceptable trial of the use of polio vaccine because supplies were short. Scarcity was adroitly used to provide valuable facts and this 'birthday lottery' was clearly justified. But if there had been enough vaccine to go round would it have been acceptable? Would it have been possible to deny the vaccine to some children in order to create a control group?*

*In clinical medicine the position is even more delicate. The doctor will persuasively break a control group in order to ensure that his patient shall have the best possible chance of survival or comfortable living. In practice, of course, scarcities do force clinical selection, but a formalized code of choice is intolerable to the doctor who feels that he must be free to make each selection an individual decision. These individual decisions are not easy to make; to assess their value is virtually impossible. To decide whether to save the life of an elderly man who will return to lead a reasonably independent life in his home or that of a young disabled boy who will need constant care is inevitably a subjective choice. Figures based on such personal variables cannot be compared. Though the cost of a treatment can be calculated, to assess its effectiveness is almost impossible.*

*Even when facts have been obtained, as occasionally they are, their message is often overridden by public pressure or medical enthusiasm for a new advance. Screening for cancer and dialysis are two examples of this irrational, but sometimes successful, allocation of resources. Medicine is less susceptible than other public activities to the application cost-analysis, and where so many things are difficult to quantify, statistical techniques can play only a limited part. For a long time to come medical priorities are likely still to be settled on the admittedly arbitrary basis of habit and tradition.*

8

# Haemodialysis and organ transplantation

R. Y. CALNE
MA, MS, FRCS
*Professor of Surgery*
*University of Cambridge*

# Haemodialysis and organ transplantation[1]

## Introduction

THERE are now many texts and a huge literature on tissue transplantation. The scientific background is exceptionally wide, stretching from protein chemistry and serology to surgical technique and including most of the disciplines of medicine and pathology. Theory and laboratory speculations have often been out of phase with clinical practice. The objective of organ transplantation differs in no way in principle from that of established medical therapy, it is to restore to a happy and useful life patients doomed to premature death from fatal disease of a vital organ. The cardinal feature of organ transplantation is that the function of the diseased organ is replaced by a biologically active graft. The large numbers of young people dying from renal disease has been a powerful stimulus to progress in organ transplantation. The surgical technique was developed sixty years ago, so to the clinician, graft rejection has been a frustrating humiliation; a poorly understood biological nuisance acting as a barrier against potential therapy. Drs Murray, Merrill, and their colleagues at the Peter Bent Brigham Hospital in Boston chose the one situation where the barrier was defective for their early studies of kidney transplantation. They demonstrated more than fifteen years ago that excellent treatment could result from a kidney grafted between identical twins. Since most people dying of fatal organ disease do not have the luxury of a perfect twin donor, the early experience in Boston served to increase efforts directed towards

1. This paper is largely reproduced from the Introduction of the essay 'Ethics and the law' by Professor Calne published in *Clinical Organ Transplantation*, Calne, R. Y. (ed.) (Blackwells).

understanding and overcoming graft rejection. Unfortunately the body has no discriminatory powers in its natural mechanisms for eliminating foreign invaders. Potentially lethal bacteria and viruses are dealt with in the same way as life-saving tissue grafts. Although to the transplanter this may be infuriating, it is perhaps not surprising. A highly efficient and effective apparatus designed to overcome infection is of obvious survival advantage in evolutionary selection. It happens that this basic biological attribute operates by an exquisitely sensitive recognition ability that mounts a continuous surveillance of all the body constituents, admitting without protest all products belonging to the individual, but immediately recognizing and reacting against any foreign material. The immunity apparatus can detect differences in the biochemical constitution of the cell membrane, that are beyond the capabilities of analytical chemists. Thus the histocompatibility differences between individuals of the same species are recognized and behave as sensitizing antigens.

Efforts to overcome rejection have been crude and empirical. Moreover most work devoted to the subject has been on skin grafts in rodents and it was subsequently found that skin is the most difficult tissue to protect from rejection and immunosuppressive agents effective in rodents did not necessarily have similar actions in man and vice versa. Despite prognostications of gloom and allegations of irresponsibility from some transplantation immunologists, surgeons proceeded to transplant kidneys in man, basing their immunosuppressive regimen on results obtained in the dog. The results have been in excess of the most optimistic hopes of the transplanters. Since every patient surviving with a functioning graft would otherwise be dead or blocking a dialysis space and thereby preventing others from receiving treatment, a survival rate of around 50 per cent at two years for grafts from cadavers and approaching 80 per cent when the donor was a close relative, must be considered even by the most bitterly prejudiced opponents of transplantation as worthwhile treatment. Certainly it compares favourably with the results of much effort devoted to the treatment of many forms of cancer. Techniques are now available to transplant every organ, but for a variety of reasons the results of kidney transplantation are at present much the best.

There are only three possible donor sources for clinical organ transplantation, namely live animals, live humans, and dead humans. It is most unlikely that organ transplantation across species will be a practical possibility until there is almost full control of the rejection process within a species. This is unfortunate, since the concept of breeding germ-free animals to varying required sizes for organ grafting into man is attractive. Entirely normal organs could be grafted with minimal ischaemic damage and many of the present ethical difficulties would be eliminated.

Live humans can only be donors of one of a pair of vital organs, for example the kidney. There are many reasons for preferring not to interfere with a healthy normal individual in order to provide a donor kidney, nevertheless there are situations where grafting a kidney between relatives offers the best chances of success and if certain rather rigorous requirements are fulfilled, the procedure is justified. Grafting from the dead cannot hurt the donor and would seem to be the most suitable donor source at present. There are many difficulties in utilizing organs from cadavers, yet most of these could be solved if there was sufficient understanding within the medical profession and goodwill in the community.

The issue of ethics and the law relating to organ grafting needs special attention.

## Ethics and the law

The publicity that followed the first cardiac allograft in man highlighted many ethical aspects of organ grafting, yet the main result has been confusion rather than an understanding of the problems. The immense emotional excitement concerning heart grafting was eagerly exploited by the mass media and unfortunately also by some medical men. Initial unwarranted optimism and adulation were followed by bitter criticism. In particular, since the operation can be performed by any competent cardiac surgeon, the prestige for the individual and institution appeared to influence some centres in deciding to pursue heart grafting even in the absence of any previous interest or research background in the subject. Some of those who did not share in the apparent glory were particularly vindictive in their criticism and did not hesitate to denounce all transplantation in press and on the radio and television. Some of the emotive phrases such as vulture, 'human vivisector', have had a disastrous influence on all organ transplantation and undermined the public's confidence in the medical profession. If some surgeons have lacked seriousness and sufficient responsibility in their approach to transplantation, their misdemeanours are trivial compared with the prejudiced and ignorant vituperation of some of the critics, whose efforts have resulted in needless deaths of many young people awaiting kidney transplantation.

The plight of those in need of organ grafting is the main ethical problem, and it has received remarkably little attention. A community that can afford vast expenditure in arms designed to destroy, can certainly cover the relatively minor financial burden required to treat the sick by organ grafting—moreover a successful organ graft is of fiscal benefit to the state, restoring an individual to work and costing often little more, and sometimes even less than conventional palliative hospital care, with a tragic fatal end. To argue that the money could be better spent in preventive medicine or underdeveloped countries is irrelevant. Suffering from disease is not confined to poor communities. Valuable treatment, expensive in its development, will become increasingly less costly as techniques improve and then the benefits will be available to all.

It is a very sad indictment of the community in the UK that only 10 per cent of young people with terminal renal disease are receiving treatment in the form of transplantation and dialysis. More than 2,000 are dying each year without help. The Government Department of Health is spending large sums in setting up transplantation and dialysis centres, but these cannot operate adequately when donor organs do not become available. Yet there are more than enough deaths from accidents, cerebral tumour, and haemorrhage to provide all the kidneys required. The failure is a result of two main difficulties which are interrelated, namely co-operation with the profession and public understanding and confidence.

There must be few people in a civilized community, who would prefer their organs to be burned or buried after death, rather than that they should save another's life. There are, however, three points of worry:

(1) Can there be assurance that the best medical care will be utilized in their terminal illness with no thought of sparing therapeutic effort to facilitate organ donation?

(2) Will irreversible death have occurred *beyond any doubt whatsoever* before organ removal commences?

(3) If organs are used for grafting can the privacy of the bereaved relatives be respected by the mass media?

These points will now be considered further.

(1) On this first matter, experience would suggest that reassurance is fully justified. The usual result of the possibility of organ grafting being raised, is for the medical and nursing staff looking after the sick patient to redouble their efforts to try and treat him. The only fear is that these efforts can be over-enthusiastic in cases with irreversible brain damage, who may be kept 'alive' artificially. This results in the tragic situation of caring for a perfused but slowly decomposing corpse.

(2) A consideration of death, irreversible and beyond doubt is more complicated although it should be made clear that the diagnosis of death in most cases presents no difficulty. The patient is usually known to be suffering from a fatal disease. Deterioration occurs and eventually the heart stops beating and breathing ceases. If this situation persists for more than five minutes in an individual at normal body temperature, then death can be diagnosed with complete confidence. Stories of people awaking in the mortuary or a coffin have been a haunting fear to some who have asked for an artery to be incised to make sure that they are dead. At least this danger of premature burial is eliminated by being an organ donor! In the context of proposed organ removal, great care in diagnosing death is usually taken by several doctors. In the extremely unlikely event of a mistake being made, the error would be revealed and rectified by the first touch of the knife.

There are cases, often especially suitable as organ donors, where the diagnosis of death is less straightforward. These are patients who have suffered cardiac arrest or brain damage sufficient to abolish spontaneous respiration and in whom the circulation and/or pulmonary ventilation have been maintained by artificial means. The only satisfactory management of such cases is for resuscitation to be continued until brain death is apparent beyond any doubt. Thus whilst there is still any difficulty in being sure no effort is spared in trying to save the patient. Once, however, irreversible brain death is established, pursuance of resuscitative efforts can do no good, in fact the reverse is true. The patient will not benefit and his relatives will suffer or, even worse, become indifferent, when they realize that the perfused tissues they visit have no relationship to the person they once loved.

If all the following features are present then the brain must be dead beyond doubt:

(1) Fixed wide dilated pupils.

(2) Absent cerebral reflexes.

(3) Absence of spontaneous respiration in the presence of adequate $CO_2$ drive.

(4) Absent cerebral circulation demonstrated by carotid and/or vertebral angiography and/or brain scanning.

(5) A persistently flat EEG.

(6) Cessation of the retinal circulation with red cell sludging on ophthalmoscopic examination.

It is usually not necessary to perform the special tests to decide to cease resuscitation, but they can be valuable where there is difficulty, for example, in cases of barbiturate poisoning or in patients who are hypothermic. The consideration so far has had *absolutely nothing* to do with transplantation. The decision to abandon resuscitation is related *solely* to the case of the afflicted patient, once made, however, the transplantation team should be informed as soon as possible so they can prepare the instruments, operating theatre, and personnel. As soon as the donor is dead the quicker the organs are cooled and removed the more likely are they to function well after grafting.

A powerful argument has been advanced and is gaining increasing acceptance in America and on the continent of Europe, to permit organ removal from patients with established brain death —*coma dépasse*—whilst ventilation of the lungs is continued and the circulation intact. This allows the surgeon to remove the organs unhurriedly whilst they are perfused with oxygenated blood and undoubtedly improves the transplantation results. There are many doctors, however, particularly in the UK, who find this procedure of organ removal from patients with *coma dépasse* unacceptable. They argue that no matter what precautions are taken, there is still the possibility of diagnosing brain death erroneously. If, however, resuscitation is abandoned and the organs are not removed until the circulation has ceased, then the brain must be dead from ischaemia and the irreversibility of the process will have been demonstrated. Following this conventional diagnosis of death, livers have been transplanted successfully and since the liver is the most sensitive organ to ischaemic damage, with the exception of the brain itself, conventional diagnosis of death is compatible with all types of organ transplantation and has the immensely reassuring feature of *revealed* irreversibility of death that provides the public and the profession with adequate safeguards. It must be admitted, nevertheless, that the practical advantages of removing organs from 'living corpses' will produce better results.[1] The chances of making a mistake in the diagnosis of *coma dépasse* must be infinitesimal if the assessment is undertaken by experienced neurologists or neurosurgeons. There can, however, be an irrational uneasiness in the minds of many that should not be disregarded. Reassurance is only certain when brain death is *revealed*. Thus few would object to organ removal from a decapitated body, an anencephalic monster, or an individual whose whole brain has been visibly extruded after an accident, even though in each of these instances the heart were still beating and providing an adequate circulation and the lungs were ventilated mechanically. These 'living corpses' would be surely acceptable organ donors on ethical grounds. In other cases where death of the brain is established by means other than visible absence of the brain, a difference of opinion will doubtless persist amongst members of the profession and the laity, as to whether organ removal whilst there is a good circulation is or is not justifiable. To wait for circulatory arrest after cessation of resuscitation can induce misgivings in none and is compatible with good organ grafting results. The merits are obvious.

It is very sad that the charitable donation of organs after death cannot remain private. The callous disregard of the feelings of bereaved relatives by the mass media has been scarcely credible. Photographs have been published with personal information quite unrelated to the operation. In the UK where complaints have been made that this information has been obtained and published contrary to the expressed wishes of the relatives, the Press Council, one of whose functions is meant to be to protect the public from

1. Which type of donor has been used is often not specified in comparisons of organ transplantation results from different centres—a serious omission, since *coma depasse* cases from the point of view of ischaemic damage are 'live' unrelated donors.

such abuses, has twice rejected the complaints on the grounds that publishing the material was in the general 'public interest'. The result, as could be anticipated, has been a reluctance on the part of bereaved relations to give permission for organ removal from the deceased's next of kin, specifically because of the fear of publicity, which the doctors cannot prevent and the Press Council has condoned. How little sympathy have those responsible for the young patients suffering from kidney disease, who have died needlessly and their tragically bereaved relatives.

## The law

In most countries, legislation relating to the disposal of dead bodies has not been framed to facilitate organ grafting. In some states, such as the UK, the law is confused on several important matters that have not so far been tested. It is unlikely that there will be sufficient organs for grafting until it is regarded as routine practice by the public and the profession for organs to be removed from all suitable cadaver donors. Then no doubt the mass media would lose interest and organ removal from corpses would be no more newsworthy than a coroner's autopsy—which is compulsory by law and is seldom objected to by individuals or public opinion and is not a subject of detailed ghoulish discussion.

In the UK, unless the donor in his lifetime had clearly expressed his wish to be an organ donor after death, it is necessary to obtain permission from the relatives. Moreover, if the case is under the jurisdiction of the coroner, his consent must also be obtained. Frequently, relatives and/or the coroner cannot be contacted in the short time available before irreversible ischaemic damage will have occurred to the organs required. Thus many organs are wasted when, in fact, it later transpires that both the patient in his lifetime and his relatives would have wished them to be used. Doctors looking after dying patients often refuse to inform the transplantation team for fear that the request to the relatives will cause them further unnecessary distress. This can be true—especially in cases of sudden unexpected death, but the reverse is by no means rare. A not unusual reply is—'I am glad you asked doctor because I am sure he would have wished it and then perhaps some good thing may come from our personal tragedy.'

In Sweden, Denmark, France, Italy, and Israel permission from the relatives is not required. This is probably the only form of legislation that will permit satisfactory development of organ grafting. Contracting into a scheme of voluntary donation would never produce sufficient response, although it would be helpful.

A reasonable legislative framework could be constructed on the following lines.

(1) *The individual's wishes should be respected* so that any who did not want their organs used for grafting would register an objection on behalf of themselves and/or their children. Suitable machinery would be set up to record and retrieve this information. This should present no serious problems of computerization. It would be necessary for the names of objectors to be determined by a hospital at any time—day or night. As an added precaution, objectors could carry a card on their person stating their wishes. It should be possible to specify organs with regard to permission and also for an individual to change his mind at any time. Those feeling strongly that they wished to be organ donors could 'contract in' under the same scheme.

(2) *If active objection had not been made—permission would be assumed.* After death—established by traditional criteria—namely cessation of the circulation and spontaneous respiration, organs could be removed. Permission from the relatives would not be necessary, but if they were available they would certainly be consulted as to the deceased's wishes and should the relatives object, their feelings would be respected, since this would be the only humane action.

(3) If it was felt desirable to remove organs whilst the circulation continued after *coma dépasse* had been diagnosed, permission of the relatives after full explanation would be necessary even in cases where the patient had 'contracted in' as a donor. In such cases signatures from two consultants experienced in neurology and/or neurosurgery should testify brain death.

(4) The potential donor in his lifetime should not be interfered with in any way not specifically directed towards his own treatment for purposes of transplantation except for removal of a few millilitres of blood for tissue typing. He should not be moved to another hospital to facilitate organ removal unless he had specifically requested that this were done.

(5) Doctors *not* concerned with the transplantation operation should care for the donor, decide if and when to abandon resuscitation, if resuscitative measures had been taken and diagnose death.

(6) In cases coming under the jurisdiction of the coroner, arrangements with the coroner and/or his pathologist, should allow organ removal to proceed, this forming part of the coroner's autopsy examination. The surgeon removing the organs would report in detail to the coroner any relevant findings. In certain cases, which would be infrequent, where organ removal might interfere with establishing the cause of death, the coroner's pathologist should partake in the operation.

(7) Publicizing the names of donors by the mass media would be unlawful even if the relatives wished it. Any complaint of an irregularity occurring would be reported to the coroner, who would then hold a public inquest.

This framework of proposed legislation would probably be acceptable to the public of most civilized communities providing accurate information was fully available. No matter what laws are devised, eventually doctors have to make decisions based on their knowledge and experience and the only real safeguard is the trust of the public in the integrity of the medical profession. Such trust is an essential feature of all clinical practice. Operative or medical treatment given for any illness implies a bond of trust between the patient and his doctor that the treatment is necessary. Moreover, it will be underlaken by the doctor conscientiously to the best of his ability. The same confidence is necessary in all aspects of transplantation surgery relating both to the donor and the recipient.

### LIVE DONORS

It is suggested that with an adult close blood relative medically suitable and of a good tissue match with the recipient, if failure to donate a kidney would lead to a genuine feeling of deprivation, then to proceed is justified. The law in the UK does not provide for organ donation from live volunteers, which technically constitutes an assault. It is, however, most unlikely that this could ever be successfully upheld in court.

### THE RECIPIENT

Provided fatal disease of a vital organ has failed to respond to conventional treatment—if there are no obvious contra-indications and an organ graft would seem to be a feasible form of treatment, then it is surely correct to bring this possibility to the patient's attention. In most cases, however, the patient will have already requested an organ transplant. It is important that the current situation is carefully explained to the patient, including the attendant risks. If after careful consideration the patient and his relatives wish to proceed then this is the correct course. A similar argument is used to decide whether or not to perform all major risky surgery. If death is 100 per cent certain in a few weeks without treatment, and organ grafting has only a 5 per cent chance of restoring the patient to a normal life for a year, then the patient should be given that chance if he wishes. Fortunately, as has been described in early chapters, the chances are much better than 5 per cent with most organ grafts.

## The future

Transplantation is already an established and valuable therapeutic procedure for kidney disease and has helped a number of patients dying from liver and heart diseases. There can be no doubt that the results will continue to improve and more organs will be successfully transplanted.

If the confidence of the public is restored so that new legislation can be introduced to help provide more organs, many young people now dying could be restored to a happy and healthy existence. Advances in tissue typing, logistics of organ distribution, and preservation can be anticipated. If, as seems likely, safer and more specific immunosuppression is developed then clinical organ transplantation will be able to help an increasing number of people and will constitute a most valuable part of surgery.

## Summary

In the past decade, an effective form of artificial kidney treatment has been developed, which will maintain patients with no renal function in moderately good health. Concurrently, kidney transplantation has developed with empirical methods of preventing the rejection reaction which result in fairly good therapy to patients who would otherwise die; thus in a number of large centres, 56 per cent of transplants from unrelated un-tissue-typed cadaver donors are functioning at two years. The longest survivor in this category is now about eight years. With living related donors, where tissue match is likely to be much better, the results at two years are around 80 per cent transplant survival and the longest surviving patient with functioning transplant is twelve years. It has now become obvious to almost all doctors caring for patients with kidney disease that the combination of dialysis and transplantation offers the best treatment for the patient with renal failure. They are not rival forms of treatment but complementary. Dialysis facilities at transplantation centres have now been established throughout the UK but at present are only treating a small minority of patients in need. From the Registrar-General's Statistical Report, it is apparent that between 2,000 and 3,000 people between the ages of 5 and 55 die each year in England and Wales from kidney disease and about 200 or 300 of these patients are being treated. Dialysis and renal transplantation although expensive are not exhorbitant in terms of other types of medical treatment and patients successfully manage return to normal life and can be gainfully employed and are therefore an economic asset to the country.

The main stumbling block in providing treatment for all is the shortage of donor organs. A whole variety of reasons have produced this shortage but the goodwill of the public is probably in general in favour of help. Changes in the law, the attitudes of certain coroners and more factual information to the public and medical profession could improve the situation.

Transplantation of other organs is at a much earlier developmental stage. Progress has been retarded chiefly because of the lack of facilities comparable to the artificial kidney to maintain a patient suffering, for example, from heart or liver disease.

Nevertheless, some good results have been obtained in transplants of both these organs and further progress is to be expected since results presently obtained with the heart and liver are in fact better than those obtained with kidney grafting ten years ago.

# DISCUSSION

*The difference between transplant surgery and other medical advances is that it requires a donor as well as a patient. Often this donor is himself a patient, and his right to however slender a chance of life must be stringently guarded.*

*Victims of road accidents, many of whom are unfortunately healthy young people, are especially suitable potential donors. Many of these with severe head injuries will respond to modern resuscitative methods. A few will have clearly suffered irreversible brain damage, but about half of these will also have suffered such hypoxic insults that their organs are unsuitable as transplants. In others brain damage, though severe, is less certainly irreversible. For them a time comes when a decision must be taken whether resuscitation should stop. For the neurologist prognostication in these circumstances is never easy and the possibility that his patient will be used as a donor makes his position more anxious. Yet it is in this group of patients that donors must be found, because for a heart or liver transplant only the organ of a patient on whom resuscitation has been attempted and abandoned is suitable. For kidney transplants the problem is less difficult, for the kidney may be removed up to $1\frac{1}{2}$ hours after the donor's death.*

*The transplant surgeon does not wish to intervene in this delicate situation until the decision to stop resuscitation has been made. But once the decision has been taken, he asks that he should be informed at once. At present he feels that after an incident which receives over-enthusiastic publicity in the press for some months he meets with more reluctance and less co-operation than his patients deserve.*

9

# Aspects of geriatric care where conflict or doubt arises

W. FERGUSON ANDERSON
OBE, MD, FRCP
*Professor of Geriatric Medicine*
*University of Glasgow*

# Aspects of geriatric care where conflict or doubt arises

## Introduction

BROTHERSTON (2) commented that demographic change in the development from a comparatively young society produced by the large Victorian birth-rate to a society with a more normal proportion of elderly—the so-called ageing society—still seems to take us by surprise. Although its emergence was inevitable and had been publicized and discussed for many years, it was extraordinary that there should still be a prevailing atmosphere almost of grievance that this had happened and astonishment that in its train had come an increasing number of frail and elderly people and chronic sick for whom society must make provision. '. . . Perforce, we must come to terms with the fact that the aged are here to stay, and in increasing numbers; this is the kind of society we live in. Two things seem certain. Nothing will really flow smoothly in the Health Service until we reach an adequate stage of provision in our society for the elderly. This means many things apart from hospital beds. The other is that a major phenomenon of the elderly *vis-à-vis* the Health Service is underdemand not overdemand. Later generations of elderly may benefit in health having been nurtured in earlier years in a better environment. They will not be so stoic in the face of disability or so unwisely sparing of the medical services as are our contemporary veterans.'

The Registrar-General's estimated total population for 1968 projected for the twenty years to 1988 shows that while there is a general increase in both the absolute numbers and the proportion of the elderly in the general population, this increase is most marked in those aged 75 and over—the most vulnerable as well as the frailest members of the community. In addition, of the population

75 years of age and over, approximately two-thirds will be females—137,000 in 1968 as compared with 186,000 in 1988. When expectation of life figures are examined between 1901 and 1966 it can be seen that women are surviving longer than men and that this gap appears to be widening. These elderly female patients make considerable demands on the services because of the degree of care required owing to their frailty and, moreover, when they are admitted to hospital they stay for a longer time than their male counterparts. Single and widowed elderly women occupy hospital beds longer than married women. In old age the proportion of widowed women increases markedly. While two-thirds of men 65 years and over are married, less than one-third of women 65 years and over are still married. The survival of the women means not only a longer time in hospital when they are ill but that in their own home there tends to be lack of support from husband or other relatives and thus a wide spectrum of expensive domiciliary services is required and, in addition, heavy pressure is placed on sheltered housing, homes for the physically or mentally frail outside the NHS, and, of course, hospital beds for those becoming ill. In regard to the domiciliary services, in most large cities there are four times as many older women living alone as there are men. The ill male is more acceptable in his own home or in the community outside the hospital and if of reasonable social habit has no difficulty in finding someone to care for him. There is certainly in Scotland an increasing number of women 75 years and over going into mental hospitals as well as increased numbers of men, with the women markedly in excess of the men. Women are occupying long-stay hospital beds for long periods before their deaths and this is perhaps the most important single problem in hospital geriatric practice today.

## 'The young old'

At a World Health Organization Conference in Kiev in 1963 (7), a new classification was suggested for the elderly. This involved calling people middle-aged (45–59), elderly (60–74), and aged (75 and over). This seems a very important decision as there is no doubt that in most developed countries a problem is posed by increasing numbers of people between 55 and 75 who are retired compulsorily, and they are often very fit. These people have really no place in our modern society and at the moment are debarred by financial restriction from work to any great extent. It would seem that correct planning for this group of older individuals might well reduce the incidence of physical and mental illness in the higher age-range. There are innumerable part-time posts which these people can fill with great satisfaction and perform a most useful duty for the community. They are particularly good at soothing problems over because of their excellent personal relations with other people, and examples of this come quickly to mind. They could provide politeness and courtesy in industry, shops, and hospitals which are so sadly lacking in this modern society.

## An experiment in re-employment

A part-time employment bureau for the retired was inaugurated by the Glasgow Retirement Council in April 1967. This consisted of an office open every afternoon during the week in the centre of Glasgow staffed by volunteers in the older age-group, who incidentally have themselves benefited greatly from the work. The scheme was launched at a time of high unemployment for men (5·9 per cent) in Glasgow and many difficulties were forecast. From the beginning, no-one concerned with this venture had any doubt that many retired men and women would welcome part-time work. This belief has been amply justified as 1,184 men and women have applied to be registered and those registering include company directors and men and women with professional qualifications as well as tradesmen and so-called 'unskilled categories'.

It has been found that men who have held senior executive posts realize that after they have retired they cannot expect to find part-time jobs at the same level of responsibility. In any case, they do not want jobs which will give them worry. While willing to work unpaid for a charitable organization, if they are working for a commercial undertaking they want to be paid for the job.

Any contact with trade-union officials has been most pleasant and they have encouraged continuance of the work.

Since April 1967, 537 retired people have obtained part-time employment. Some examples are: 95 men and 26 women in clerical work, 46 men as messengers, 20 men as handymen, 20 for security work, 13 women have been employed as companion helps, and 8 as book-keeper/cashiers.

Is interest in employment anything to do with medicine? Has the physician in geriatric medicine a duty to try and keep people secure and of sound mental health? Has the doctor a place in society as a leader of labour policies—bearing in mind that there is in being in our country an NHS?

## Retirement

For the first time in the social history of the world men and women are retiring from their life's work when they are still physically and mentally fit. More than 1,000 such people retire each day in the UK and the present trend in redundancy and retirement policies means that this figure will increase dramatically. Heron and Chown (5) stated that compulsory retirement provided a striking example of the way in which an arbitrary choice made in one era of social and medical history can become fixed despite later changes. In investigating the mental health of older people, it has come to be accepted that for many compulsory retirement is not of advantage. For the well-educated and those prepared to think about retirement before it happens, compulsory retirement is probably no great evil. For those who have not thought about it and who have been used to routine work without the advantage of many hobbies or interests, compulsory retirement has many disadvantages. The question may be posed if the lack of incentive to earn money and have a purpose in life in the young old man, for example 60 to 65, precipitates feelings of uselessness and depression which may lead to physical and mental illness and eventually to death. When the men die, do the surviving women, because of adverse factors—lack of affection, companionship, and interest—become ill physically or mentally and, because they are stronger, do not die but remain as chronic invalids?

Surely there is an urgent need for a complete review of retirement policies. It might be thought that a much wider study is required of, for example, the total labour force necessary in the country, the hours of work per week which individuals should undertake, and that planning should be initiated to include the skill and aptitudes of those who are in the upper age-range. It is suggested that opportunities for retraining for change of employment in the same area of work which the individuals have followed in their life should be provided on a voluntary basis between the ages of 50 and 55. Following this, if the person desires, regular part-time employment should be offered three or four days per week from 55 years on until the individual feels that he or she is no longer willing or able to undertake this work. Final cessation from work would be in most cases around the age of 70 and conditions of service should be the same for both sexes. This prolonged period of part-time employment would enable the individual to adjust and prepare for full retirement. Experience in this field or retraining of older people has shown that even a slight change of occupational routine requires to be done in a precise and detailed way. This retraining would ensure employment which is less arduous and involves less responsibility and give more time for leisure. It is also likely that the stimulus of an alteration in the routine of life would promote an improvement in the mental health of the individual. Adequate pensions would require to be paid by right at 55 years and money earned by part-time employment subject only to income tax deduction.

## Pre-retirement training

In Glasgow, since October 1959, 610 women and 2,077 men have attended 162 day-release courses in preparation for retirement. In September 1969, a graduate reunion conference was held with some 200 men and women who had experienced five to ten years of retirement since attending their courses between October 1959 and June 1965. Ten study groups of twenty were formed and full discussions followed. From such experience, although in fact the numbers are very small, it can be stated that for the older person such courses seem to be of value and as the work proceeds so more information is obtained. Living in retirement courses have now been commenced and these provide great opportunities for people to meet and for companionship and interest to be furthered.

## Housing policies

A new attitude to the care of the elderly is essential in trying to provide some prospect of happiness and hope in old age. The elderly about to retire from their life work should have something to look forward to, certainly the older woman who has just lost her husband requires some way of maintaining her mental health. The new idea of widespread provision of protected or warden-supervised housing is one method by which the individual who has been bereaved can be helped. This type of housing is also suitable although not needed so much for the married couple with too large a home who could move into a smaller protected house. The basic principle in this sort of provision is to encourage older people to fend for themselves, while at the same time providing a protected environment. There is a warden or caretaker constantly on duty and when this person has to have free time then one of the fitter old people in the community is encouraged to act as caretaker. In the initial stage of choosing the tenants for such houses, it is wise to pick some of the younger old and encourage them to take an interest in those who are much frailer, thus instilling a policy of good neighbourliness from the start. Such housing should have top-grade intercommunication systems which enable the person sitting in the warden's office to be in contact with the other members of the community who are in their own homes. It is possible that even slightly confused individuals could continue to live in such an environment if it was appropriately planned.

Homes for the mildly mentally disturbed are also urgently required. Admission would take place only after initial psychosocial medical assessment. It is relevant to note that Whitehead (6) is of the opinion that a large number of old people in psychiatric hospitals could be discharged if they had somewhere to go.

Public opinion is in advance of many doctors' views in desiring an improvement in the quality of life for older people. Medical training is not orientated to early diagnosis of disease in old people. The psychosocial conditions of the patients have not always been fully appreciated by some physicians who seem to desire that physical illness should be considered as an element apart—a scientific subject untrammelled by mind or environment. Surely these considerations must have stimulated such legislation as the Social Work (Scotland) Act. Perhaps the dichotomy imposed by the NHS on many medical teachers, dividing home care and hospital treatment, is responsible in part for this outlook. Undergraduate medical training should encourage a realistic approach to the psychological and social factors incurred with loss of health and to their special importance in the elderly. There is constant need to ensure that the student learns to communicate with his patient. Gillis (4) observed that in medical and ancillary practice there are those who through lack of knowledge of the mechanics of human behaviour or the inability to use such knowledge together with inadequacy of learned skill in relationships are unable to evaluate successfully psychosocial problems. Perhaps too widespread a use of multiple choice questions with 'Yes/No' answers may inhibit the medical student's power to express himself.

## Health centres

As a result of work undertaken at the Kilsyth Health Centre near Glasgow, it is hoped to introduce a scheme whereby trained health visitors will visit in the first instance people 70 years and over in the community served by the Health Centre. The age of 70 has been chosen because at that time there is a marked increase in morbidity and those who would benefit from some form of health visitor's screening are much more numerous. The health visitor would report back to the GPs, and it has also been suggested that in a group of five GPs one would be specially trained in geriatric medicine to give advice to the other members of the group but not to see all the old people in the practice who would attend their own doctors. In such a scheme, the actual number of elderly people requiring routine medical, psychological, and social assessment by the doctor is few as most of the people can be screened quite accurately by the health visitor who can report back to the Centre with the findings. This procedure of seeking out older people has been adopted because of the unsatisfactory results obtained by the self-reporting of illness in the elderly. Socially isolated old people who live alone have real difficulty in obtaining aid; many elderly people deny illness using a mental mechanism almost unconsciously to resolve emotional conflict and minimize anxiety by denying the existence of an important health defect. Lastly, many older people attribute to ageing itself the symptoms and signs of disease—here perhaps depression so common in the elderly plays a part.

It is hoped that the physician in geriatric medicine will visit such health centres one day per week to provide the GPs with the service which they require. Two services are suggested—one which would consist in supervising the work done by the health visitor in conjunction with the GPs in ascertaining the people who are at risk in the community, for example, as suggested above, by visiting those 70 years and over and by compiling an accurate register of the elderly; the second would be in running an early diagnostic clinic in the health centre and seeing patients referred by the GPs. Co-ordination of local domiciliary services at the health centre would ensure that necessary services, often inexpensive, were provided to enable the older person to remain at home as long as possible. It is also expected that if such a scheme worked properly, it would soon be possible to visit those in a younger age-group than the people 70 years and over. In any society, the amount of money available for the care of any group of people is limited and under the new Social Work Act it seems essential to realize that any call for a social service is often a call for medical assistance also and the old person who requires a home help or meals-on-wheels or requests admission to an old person's home will amost certainly, as well as social need, have medical need. Thus, a request for help should be regarded as a time when a complete medical psychosocial assessment of the old person should be made. Every effort must be made by accurate selection to ensure that only those requiring a service are given the correct facility, for example, meals-on-wheels or home help. Bearing in mind the Williams' report, more and more local authorities are arranging for courses of instruction for home helps and it has been suggested that each local authority should have in addition a cadre of specially trained home helps who might be able to care for those elderly people who are mentally confused, and after a proper assessment of the patient such a home help might be of great value.

The appropriate service must be provided using, wherever possible, the right person. There will always be a significant disparity between the volume of old people's needs and the number of professional and voluntary workers available to meet these needs. However, this must not inhibit proper planning, and in defence of expenditure it has to be noted that it must always be cheaper to a health service if patients live and die untreated (8).

The final aim of the health centre in regard to old people is that the whole spectrum of help required by the older individual should be available at one place. In time, there seems no reason why a representative of the Social Security department should not be present there also. It would be of great assistance to many elderly people if representatives of the clergy would visit the health centre at stated times. Why is each person who is entitled to benefit under the NHS not given a little booklet with an outline of the way to obtain the help he or she requires and with a list of the clinics which are in being at the local health centre? Brockington and Lempert (1) surveyed the over-80s in Stockport and found that many old people in need are unaware of the help available and that the efforts of the various agencies, unofficial and official, are unco-ordinated.

## Area health boards

If old people are to be properly cared for under the scheme of area health boards there will require to be the closest co-operation between the social work department and the physician in geriatric medicine and the GPs. The social work department should be represented in each hospital and in each health centre to encourage continuity of care. Once an old person has been found to be unwell supervision should be continuous, and certainly all the people discharged from hospital should be followed up by a health visitor, district nurse, or social worker. Much effort of clinical service in hospital is wasted by inadequate after-care, as demonstrated in Scotland by Ferguson and MacPhail (3). Many problems remain and co-ordination of activity is usually the answer if such can be obtained. For example, the rehousing of an old person from slum property to a new house in an area where she knows no one and is now remote from her friends and neighbours is not an act of kindness to the old person but in fact a disservice. Such an elderly person will not enjoy her new house but will become depressed and unhappy. Thus, rehousing is a very delicate and difficult problem which should be handled bearing in mind the friends and neighbours that have existed in a local community. The quality of housing, while desperately important to old people, is not the only one factor essential to their mental health. In the education of doctors and social workers and nurses, it is obvious that in a society where most of the requests for help will come from the elderly instruction in their proper care should be available.

In conclusion, population trends have revealed the near immortality of the elderly woman. The unsatisfactory mental health of many old people has been attributed in part to retirement policies. If men lived longer, perhaps the unhappiness of many elderly women would be lessened. Seeking out of illness in the upper age-range has been discussed with a plea for co-ordination of services and the continuing attempt to supply the correct type of help to the individual in need. Stress has been laid on the need for undergraduate training not only in the care of the elderly but also in the art of communicating with patients and of applying scientific knowledge to the medical psychosocial assessment of the ill.

## REFERENCES

1. Brockington, F., and Lempert, S. M. (1966). *The Social Needs of the Over Eighties* (Manchester: Manchester University Press).
2. Brotherston, J. H. F. (1969). 'Change and the National Health Service', *Scott. med. J.* **14,** 130.
3. Ferguson, T., and MacPhail, A. N. (1954). *Hospital and Community* (London: Oxford University Press).
4. Gillis, L. (1962). *Human Behaviour in Illness* (London: Faber & Faber).
5. Heron, A., and Chown, Sheila (1967). *Age and Function* (London: Churchill).
6. Whitehead, A. (1970). *Hospital Management.* Geriatric Care Supplement (Sept./Oct.), p. 419.
7. WHO Regional Office for Europe (1963). *Report on a Seminar on the Health Protection of the Elderly and the Aged and the Prevention of Premature Ageing, Kiev, 14–22 May* (Copenhagen).
8. Office of Health Economics (1964). *New Frontiers in Health* (London: Office of Health Economics).

# 10

# The implications of present practices in geriatrics

*Advances in medical science*
*tend to convert acute*
*into long-term*
*disabling conditions*

M. ROTH
MD, FRCP, DPM
*Professor of Psychological Medicine*
*University of Newcastle upon Tyne*
*and Member of the Nuffield Provincial*
*Hospitals Trust's Consultative Committee*

# The implications of present practices in geriatrics

*Advances in medical science tend to convert acute into long-term disabling conditions*

THE ageing of populations is a major challenge confronting highly developed countries in every part of the world. It tends to be forgotten that it reflects considerable social, economic, and medical achievement. It arises from two main factors. The first is the decline in mortality rate for a wide variety of conditions. The second is the decline in birth-rate which results in a relative increase of the proportion in higher age-groups. However, although death-rates have declined in a number of segments of the life span, life expectation in old age has changed little over the past fifty years, particularly in men. The progress of medical science will probably change this and will also reduce the high mortality resulting from a number of disorders in middle life. The problems of the aged will then expand further. The point is that the so-called 'burdens' of old age which all highly developed communities are trying to tackle at the present, are the obverse side of the coin of social and medical progress. We cannot have our affluence and wish away the problems of the aged.

The points made are illustrated with particular clarity by recent advances in medical science. During the past twenty-five to thirty years these have rarely had the effect of eliminating at one fell swoop one or more seriously disabling medical conditions. The more usual effect has been to convert some acute or rapidly progressive disease into one that gives rise to disability extending over a longer period of years. Medical science tends to mitigate rather than cure illnesses, to prolong life rather than to restore a state of complete health. The most complete successes are those achieved when the disabled person can survive into old age and be in a position to benefit from geriatric care. The ultimate purpose of paediatrics is to make geriatrics feasible.

The problems of old age enter in this way into every equation that expresses a major contemporary socio-medical issue. If we wish to improve the outcome of hypertension, cardiovascular, and cerebrovascular disease, which take such a terrible toll of middle-aged males in all advanced countries, we shall almost certainly do so by slowing down the rate of progress of these conditions thus permitting the sufferers to survive and qualify as geriatric problems. If we wish to achieve better population control, we can do so only at the cost of decreasing birth-rates and thus increasing the relative proportion of aged people in the population. Elimination of the socio-economic gap between the haves and the have-nots will narrow the differential in life-expectation between the classes and thus increase the relative proportion of the aged. If we are to achieve a better prognosis for those who are chronically dependent on alcohol or heavy cigarette smoking we can do so only at the expense of promoting the survival into late life of many of those who die at present in middle age. And if we are to develop improved treatment of depressive illness and of suicidal tendencies we would prolong the life of many people only to suffer more attacks of depression and make further suicidal attempts at a later stage in the life-span.

The only conceivable way in which we might have our cake and eat it would be to arrest the progress of medicine, that is to impose a moratorium on all forms of medical research, except perhaps those that are concerned with arriving at the best possible exploitation of existing knowledge. Such a moratorium on all inquiries that might control the ageing process has in fact been recommended by some workers. But such policies would quickly run up against the fact that the conditions that parody the ageing process, the senile forms of degenerative disease, almost certainly commence in earlier life. And their progress is hastened by some of the main scourges of middle age such as cardiovascular disease, cerebrovascular disease, and diabetes. Scientific inquiry into these problems would also have to be terminated.

There is, therefore, no practical and humane solution that will enable us to evade the problems of old age. Besides there is far too much to be learnt from them. Even if the care of those who have contributed substantially to our existing affluence were not a compelling moral obligation, it would be short-sighted to divert scientific attention from geriatrics and gerontology. No sharp separation is possible between the many disabling conditions of later life and the disorders of middle age that cause many premature deaths and leave other patients with residual disabilities requiring medical and social care over long periods. 'Premature' refers to the sudden termination at 40 of a valuable and productive life because a pump ceases to work.

## Care of the aged in community and institutions

In considering the type of provision to be made for those who are disabled, certain distinctions are important. Evidence from the Newcastle survey has demonstrated that, although the family is frequently willing and able to provide the care needed for physical incapacity, with the advent of serious mental disturbance, particularly persistent mental confusion, restless and disturbed behaviour and incontinence, a number of families prove incapable of carrying the burden and are compelled to request institutional care for their relative.

There is an important distinction here between those with and those without cerebral degenerative disease. That those with cerebral disease make far larger demands on the hospital services was shown by a recent study in Newcastle (3). In a random sample of 758 cases, 5·8 per cent of people had arteriosclerotic and senile dementia. Follow-up studies over 2½–4 years showed that these accounted for more than 50 per cent of the time spent by the ageing in residential homes, for 46 per cent of the time spent in geriatric beds, and 34 per cent of the time spent by the whole sample in hospital beds. Compared with a carefully matched control group of old people without mental illness, but with a great deal of physical disability, they had spent four times as long in hospital, and ten times as long in residential homes. Under existing circumstances, this lengthy occupation of beds in institutions and hospitals could not have been avoided without serious burdens on the family, particularly in working-class homes.

## The contribution of the family

Yet 95·5 per cent of elderly people subsist somehow in their own or relatives' homes. Townsend and Wedderburn (5) reported that four times as many bedfast or otherwise severely incapacitated old people were living at home, as in all types of institutions. They also found that of those who were ill in bed for some time in the course of a year, 70 per cent relied on a spouse (also elderly), children, or other relatives for help with housework, 80 per cent for help with shopping, and 82 per cent for provision of meals. The health and welfare services would be helpless without this family contribution. This is made abundantly clear by estimates of the size of the mental health problem derived from epidemiological studies.

Thus a recent survey of psychiatric illness in a random community sample of elderly people living at home in the North of England (2), showed that 10·3 per cent of them suffered from degenerative cerebral disease and, in about half of these, the mental deterioration was as severe as in cases normally found in mental hospital, yet fewer than one-fifth of them were in either a hospital or a home. In addition, 34 per cent suffered from affective disorder, and in 12·5 per cent it was of at least moderate severity.

Grad and Sainsbury (1) found that, although a community-orientated service entailed greater burdens for the family than a conventional hospital-based one, many relatives generally preferred the former to sending their aged folk away.

The maintenance of the family group living in close proximity should therefore be a major consideration in future planning because the present situation is precarious. For although 95·5 per cent of old people live at home, mostly by family help, the remaining 4·5 per cent is putting serious pressure on the health and welfare services. Even an additional 1 per cent would have a catastrophic effect. There is, however, no guarantee that such an increase will not occur in the foreseeable future, because of social pressures and changes. When long-established industries such as mining and shipbuilding are terminated in one part of the country or when new towns are created, the greater mobility of younger people tends to place distance between them and their aged relatives. Thus social change may be eroding the means that families have employed, over many generations, for the care of their aged members, without putting any form of support in its place.

## The preservation of existing social assets

It was with a view to averting such dangers portended by recent developments that the World Health Organization stated three principles which should be borne in mind when new towns or communities are in process of development.

(1) The wishes of those whose lives are to be radically changed, by removal to a fresh environment, should be ascertained and met, as far as possible, in the community plan. Social groups should be moved together so that the propinquity of the generations remains intact.

(2) When the movement of sections of the public becomes necessary, it should be planned from the outset in collaboration with public health experts, sociologists, and experts in mental health. Consideration must be given to long-established human relationships and to the mental and physical health of those to be moved not only to issues of economics, architecture, and engineering.

(3) Since the feeling of belonging to a social group with a sense of purpose in common is known to be related to mental well-being, new settlements should be planned so that corporate effort may come about and bring with it a new sense of community and social significance.

## Attitudes to the aged

It is surely right that those whose hard work in the past laid the foundations of the affluence which we in the west now enjoy, should have a share of that affluence by being given by the community the kind of support they need whether in their own homes (where they best like to remain while it is at all possible) or in homes or hospitals.

In the remote past more summary utilitarian attitudes often decided what was done with the aged. The Romans called aged senators, Depontani, a name derived from the old Roman cry 'The men of sixty *ad pontem*'—to the bridge—from which old, worn-out, and, therefore, useless people were thrown and drowned in the river (6). Among nomadic and primitive peoples the aged and disabled were often disposed of or they would, according to a well-established convention, dispose of themselves.

Sir James Frazer related how Fiji islanders, because they believed that their permanent state in Elysium would be that in which they died, used to call their families together before their mental and physical powers had altogether gone, and ask to be buried alive. They were also actuated by the desire not to live to be a burden and an object of contempt (7). These practices may be contrasted with the veneration of the aged that characterized the most ancient and long-sustained civilisation in the world—that of the Chinese people. This veneration was not without its problems and gerontocracy was only one of them. But this is not relevant to the present argument. The point is that civilization is concerned with values and in Bertrand Russell's words 'with values that are independent of utility'. These same values should surely prevent active intervention to resuscitate or prolong a life which has become mindless, helpless, and painful. There is a distinction between actively terminating a life (which doctors should never do) and not intervening when life in any real sense has passed. There is a growing tendency for medical means to be used, since they are there, without consideration of the value of what they achieve.

## REFERENCES


1. GRAD, J. C., and SAINSBURY, P. (1968). 'The effects that patients have on their families in a community care and a control psychiatric service. A two-year follow-up', *Br. J. psychiat.* **114**, 265–78.

2. KAY, D. W. K., BEAMISH, P., and ROTH, M. (1964). 'Old age mental disorders in Newcastle-upon-Tyne. Part I: A study of prevalence', ibid. **110**, 146–58.

3. —— BERGMANN, K., FOSTER, E. M., MCKECHNIE, A. A., and ROTH, M. (1970). 'Mental illness and hospital usage in the elderly: a random sample followed-up', *Compr. psychiat.* **2**, 26–35.

4. —— —— —— and GARSIDE, R. F. (1966). 'A four-year follow-up study of a random sample of old people originally seen in their own homes. A physical, social and psychiatric enquiry', *Proc. Fourth World Congr. psychiat., Madrid, 1966.* Excerpta Medica Congress Series, no. 150, pp. 1668–70 (Amsterdam: Excerpta Medica).

5. TOWNSEND, P., and WEDDERBURN, D. (1965). *The Aged in the Welfare State* (London: G. Bell & Sons Ltd).

6. VARRO, MARCUS TERENTIUS (116–27 B.C.). *Satirae Menippeae,* Satire Sexagesis, ll. 493 and 494–5. Collected by Bucheler, F., 4th edn, ed. by Heraeus, W. (1904) (Berlin: Weidmann).

7. VISCHER, A. L. (1947). *Old Age: Its Compensations and Rewards* (London: Allen & Unwin).

8. WORLD HEALTH ORGANIZATION (1959). *Mental Health Problems of Ageing and the Aged. Sixth Report of the Expert Committee on Mental Health.* Technical Report Series, no. 171 (Geneva: WHO).

# DISCUSSION

*Citizens in the first twenty years of their lives are not grouped together as 'the young'. They are recognized as infants, under-5s, schoolchildren, school-leavers, adolescents, and young adults. More or less adequate medical and social services are provided for each group. Too often citizens in the last twenty years of their lives are all casually grouped together as 'the old'. The over-60s contain as many entities as the under-20s, but the social and medical services for senior citizens tend to be geared to the needs of the older members of the group, and the needs of the young elderly have been largely ignored. Up to a point this is reasonable, for fit people in their 60s, and indeed in their early 70s, can still fend for themselves and are probably the better for doing so. But if they are to lead reasonable lives, they must have adequate incomes, companionship, and interests, and most of the group face the difficulties of early enforced retirement. Exposure to poverty, loneliness, and boredom can prematurely change the elderly fit into the ailing old. Though a health centre would be a suitable base for all forms of help provided for them, medical care is only a small part of the social services these people need.*

*For many the greatest help would be part-time employment, which would both allow them to earn some extra money and to keep in touch with other people.*

*In rural surroundings the elderly find part-time jobs fairly easily; the professional man probably has interests and committees which will continue; the sedentary craftsman can sometimes carry on with his job. But for the city-bound factory worker or the man engaged in strenuous physical work, things are not so easy. He may need training in new skills and he must be willing to accept a job which will be less onerous, exacting, and profitable than his old one. In Holland sheltered workshops already offer training and jobs to the elderly as well as to the mentally and physically handicapped, but this would seem to be an unsuitable and unappealing environment for them. Professor Ferguson Anderson described a small employment bureau in Glasgow which was a promising example of self-help. This might well be expanded to part-time work in the running of the social services, which, even in times of unemployment, are badly in need of extra staff and which might offer scope to such qualities as courtesy, tolerance, and kindliness.*

*But whatever solution is found, and there could be many different solutions, jobs for the elderly should be found within the framework of society, not only because there are so many of them, but also because they should be encouraged to remain part of the community.*

# 11

# Pyschopathy as a clinical entity and its management

P. D. SCOTT
MA, MD, FRCP, FRCPsych.
*Consultant Physician*
*The Maudsley Hospital*

# Psychopathy as a clinical entity and its management

NOBODY has ever demonstrated in psychopaths a pathognomonic lesion or disorder of function. Such physiological, psychological, or social correlates as exist are not of a very high order; thus even in very selected and relatively rare habitually aggressive psychopaths no less than a third have normal EEGs; there is no clear relationship with psychological characteristics; psychopaths can be found in all social classes and (according to Cleckley) even in all professions. The psychopath conforms to the rule (if to none other) that a given pattern of behaviour can be reached from a number of different directions in terms of psychopathology, motivation, or setting. Several conclusions follow: we should be cautious in accepting psychopaths entirely as a medical responsibility, or as a single clinical entity; description, classification, and epidemiological studies are still the outstanding needs in this field; and, since the only firm quality of the psychopath is his persistently aggressive or irresponsible behaviour in society, we are likely to find the more severe examples either in hospital or prisons for these are the only two basic solutions to problems of seriously embarrassing behaviour. It is obvious that society displays some ambivalence or uncertainty, as to which of these two solutions to use; Penrose has demonstrated very clearly that the extent to which they are used varies inversely.

## Hospital or prison

Many factors govern the choice between hospitals and prisons. First, the image which the institutions have acquired: hospitals carry the image of hospitable, protecting, comfortable places without stigma, for ill patients (with a recognizable disorder of function) who suffer through no fault of their own, who voluntarily submit to be passively restored to health; prisons are seen as uncomfortable, withholding places having a strong stigma, for the incarceration of antisocial persons (having no disorder of function) who have brought their suffering upon themselves through wicked behaviour which needs punishment to make them actively change their ways.

All these points are open to criticism. Historically there have been periods at which, in terms of overcrowding, stigma, and abuse of civil rights, there can have been little to choose between hospital and prison. Even until very recently some groups of hospital patients have lived in no less squalid conditions and certainly with less chance of legal redress than prisoners (2). Stigma is certainly different in the two services: in hospitals it is bunched and concentrated in the three special hospitals and to a much smaller extent these days, in subnormality and psychiatric hospitals, leaving general hospitals completely free. Prisons on the other hand have a high stigma almost uniformly distributed.

Discussion on the criteria by which illness is judged, in the present state of our knowledge, is bound to be unhelpful. Lewis (3) concludes that we have to rely on adequate performance of physiological and psychological functions and 'so far as we cannot designate formal, major functions of the human organism and lack of means of judging whether they work efficiently, we are handicapped in recognizing health and illness in a reliable and valid way'.

However this may be, unless history stands as still as the sun on Gibeon, it is certain that some conditions which we now regard as psychopathic, or as social deviancy, will in future be recognized as definite pathological entities. But quite apart from such speculation, it is only just beginning to be appreciated that a high proportion of recidivist prisoners do show criteria of illness which are often as adequate as for patients in psychiatric hospitals. West (7) found that a third of his sample of habitual prisoners had a history of severe mental disorder, and the great majority (88 per cent) were 'severely deviant in personality'. Even amongst those sentenced to prison for the first time, 10 per cent have had previous mental or subnormality hospital admission, 3 per cent are psychotic, and 14 per cent backward or subnormal; quite apart from very high levels of personality disorder (60 per cent), alcoholism (27 per cent), and sexual deviation (8 per cent) (4). Of Borstal lads, already screened for psychosis and mental subnormality, 27 per cent were found to have some form of mental abnormality (5). Of 149 boys, aged between 14 and 16 years, consecutively released from an approved school, none was mentally ill, but 60 per cent had marked personality disorders of one sort or another (the traits having been recorded before admission, apparent during their stay, and observed independently by more than one staff member) (6).

On the other hand there may be little difference, either as regards culpability, or long-term treatment needs, between patients in hospital as a direct result of excessive eating, smoking, drug-taking, dangerous driving, alcoholism, sexual promiscuity, and people who have been imprisoned on account of antisocial behaviour of comparable degree. For example it may only be on account of very minor differences in previous experience that, of two menopausal housewives, whose daughters have just got married and are appreciably depressed, one should steal and go to prison while the other swallows tablets and goes to hospital.

Quite apart from terminological and not very useful questions as to who is ill and who is not, it is abundantly clear that the prisons contain a very high proportion of inmates who are by any criteria psychopathic. Thus West divided his sample of habitual prisoners into: Non-Deviants, 12 per cent; Active-Aggressive Deviants, 36 per cent; and Passive Inadequate Deviants, 52 per cent. Silberman and Gibbens classify their sample of 306 inmates from three different prisons (each receiving principally from the London area) into: good prognosis, 30 per cent; young, severely maladjusted, 43 per cent; isolated frequently alcoholic recidivists, likely to be incapable of adjusting outside without help, 27 per cent.

Patients are often kept in psychiatric and subnormality hospitals under order, sometimes in conditions of maximum security, and it is even possible to compel physically ill patients to enter hospital (Public Health Act, 1936). Experience has shown that far less compulsory restriction of liberty is required in the hospital system than was supposed before the 1959 Mental Health Act. On the other hand within the prison system there are many completely open establishments and a very great ease of transfer both up and down the scale of security. Here, too, experience has shown that categories of inmates (e.g. drunkenness offenders at Spring Hill prison) who used to be detained in security prisons, are quite amenable under open conditions.

Most important of all, the public image of the prisons as punitive is hopelessly wrong (and who can wonder since they are officially known as Penal Establishments). No British prison is punitively intended. Offenders are sent to prison as punishment, but once there, there is no punitive intent whatever unless the inmate has been called before the governor and found to have committed a breach of the prison regulations. The prisons may be squalid in their overcrowding and outdated in their architecture, they may and often are undeniably unpleasant but this is certainly not deliberate. Unhappily the endeavours being made to relieve the squalor are constantly defeated by the ever-rising tide of the prison population (four times as large as before the war and rising still at the crippling rate of 3,000 per year).

It is thus that the common concept of the differences between hospitals and prisons is faulty. Madness and badness are not on the same parameter; the mad can be bad or saintly, and the bad can be mad or sane. Inevitably therefore since the line between patients and prisoners can never be clearly drawn so also the institutions themselves must overlap.

The second factor governing choice between hospital and prison includes *social considerations of tolerance within the community, and availability of placements.* The degree of tolerance of deviant behaviour including that due to mental defect and mental illness as well as that usually classed as criminal, is not clearly known, but probably depends to a considerable extent on such factors as the development of industry, the migration to town-dwelling, the break up of extended families and the primary social controls that exist in small communities, the encouragement of specialization in social function, the habit of looking to the welfare state to solve problems, and the vulnerability of large organizations to attack through the public media of communication, so that they are less and less able to stand up to criticism or to say 'no'. These factors make for looseness of social contacts within the community, and the less well a man knows his neighbour, the less sympathy he feels, the more defensiveness, and the more anxiety about any deviant behaviour. The public image of the prisoner or convict, and of the special hospital patient, greatly exaggerates their dangerousness.

Research into prediction of recidivism and other aspects of dangerousness should have high priority for it will enable us to apportion slender reserves, and to gain the confidence and thus raise the tolerance of the public to offenders. It is very greatly to the credit of our parole board that over a period of 2½ years only 15 of 4,178 paroled prisoners (0·3 per cent) committed further offences of a violent or sexual nature.

Criteria for the making of a diagnosis such as psychopathic personality vary with social conditions. Thus to quote from Lewis (3) in a Baltimore inquiry there was a tendency to interpret inability to earn a satisfactory living as evidence of psychopathic personality, but after experience of the industrial depression of the 1930s familiarity with the unemployment made it less of a mark of defective character and consequently the diagnosis of psychopathic personality was more rarely used. The higher and wealthier grades of society are more likely to avoid court appearances or custodial sentences, and to obtain medical treatment. While the behaviour of the individual must play the principal part in determining whether he is brought to the doctor or the magistrate, yet the particular outlook of these specialists may take over from that point, and it may be most useful to keep them in touch with one another in order that they may appreciate how often their work approaches or overlaps, and in order that therapeutic zeal may be tempered by the conflicting needs of the community and vice versa.

Magistrates must be acutely aware of the limitations of prison sentences for a wide range of the more inadequate offenders, and would gladly utilize any alternative disposals, or any special facility available. Similarly for the major offender, for example the murderer, no doubt the number of such cases dealt with by Section 2, Homicide Act, followed by a Section 60 order under the Mental Health Act, would be diminished if it were known that adequate treatment facilities were available within the prison system.

## Summarizing the argument to this point

(1) The term psychopath is more of an administrative and legal term than medical, and psychopaths cannot be regarded as entirely a medical responsibility.

(2) The prisons contain a high proportion of personality disordered persons (more inadequate than aggressive) who are indistinguishable from psychopaths, and are often grossly handicapped psychologically or psychiatrically.

(3) The public image of the functions of prisons and hospitals, and of the dangerousness of criminals is not realistic. Despite the overlap in clinical material the hospitals and prison systems are still very much apart from one another.

(4) The factors directing psychopaths to prison rather than hospitals are more arbitrary, wider, and more complex than is commonly supposed.

(5) The prisons are overfull and their complement is expected to continue to increase rapidly from the present figures of approximately 40,000.

## What is known about the best means of managing psychopaths?

We have learnt of the enormous clinical variety within this amorphous category and to respect the non-psychiatric, especially the social factors involved. At the same time we have to recognize that many of our neatest diagnoses (for example, the YY syndrome, these are sometimes very odd and psychopathic personalities) make not the least difference to the handling of the case. On the analogy (which is not entirely inept) that the patient has a limp, it does not make a very great deal of difference whether the pathological process, ten or twenty years ago, was a motor-car accident, a congenital deformity, or a touch of 'polio'; to such a person a good friend who makes him get on with the job of living, and makes him utilize his remaining assets, concentrating on the undamaged functions, may be more important than the doctor who is concerned mainly with the pathological process. This is why prison officers, probation officers, and other social workers and even voluntary associates (as they are sometimes called) are often effective, especially if they have the backing of a doctor and can call on him in any crisis or uncertainty.

We know that no single institution can cope with the problems of psychopaths; that treatment in the open, in residential institutions, and in security institutions, must all be in close liaison.

As in any other form of psychotherapy, getting the patient to want to change is the most essential and difficult part. Too often we expect him to change to our own personal image of rectitude, forgetting his social class and his personal limitations, and preferences, and almost always we expect him to effect the change at a rate which we dictate—perhaps within six months or a five-year prison sentence. If he has been dangerous, and appears to remain so, he must be in custody. What to do with him then is not always agreed. Some wait for maturity or 'burning out', making life as tolerable and as little damaging as possible in the process. Some utilize at rather a simple and authoritative level, training programmes and the 'inculcation of work habits'. Some arrange group living on intensely practical lines aiming at getting staff and patient to face the individual with his own faulty habits of response, and perhaps showing him how to adopt better ones, always offering support when the going gets too tough. Some deliberately put pressure on the patient, usually through the indeterminate custodial sentence, to identify with new aims rather after the fashion of a humanely ordered process of 'thought reform' or 'brain-washing'. What is universally agreed is that whatever is done must be in a manifestly helping and not a retributive setting, that always the patient is pushed towards accepting the realities of the situation, especially his limitations and how he can best get on with others, despite handicaps.

More and more one is forced to the conclusion that custodial care has only two purposes. First, finding out when and what sort of after-care will be appropriate; second, protecting (with as little damage to the individual as possible) the community if release is not indicated. Especially with psychopaths there is no evading the demand for personal attention; this rarely needs to be of a specialized nature, nor of a befriending nature (the psychopath is usually incapable of handling such a relationship) but always of a parental nature. Psychopaths are best understood as children, and as such they need good parent substitutes, who are concerned, always around, dependable, having sufficient know-how and maturity to be able to meet crises, able to lay down limits of behaviour, and insist on them without rejecting the 'child'. Anyone who can do this is likely to be a first-class therapist whether a civilian, a social worker, or a volunteer. But since the crises are frequently of a medical nature (threats of suicide, pill-swallowing, and psychotic or near psychotic states) it is essential for a doctor to be in the offing, if not as it were at the head of the table; thus there is nearly always a doctor in charge of the most effective psychopathic units—in this country Dr Gray at Grendon Prison, Drs Prewer and Cooper at Parkhurst Prison, Dr Craft at Garth, Dr McGrath and his colleagues in special hospitals, Dr Stuart Whiteley at the Henderson Hospital, Dr O'Connell at the Northgate Clinic, and many others.

There are different views about the desirability of an indeterminate sentence; some say it is essential and others not; all would agree that some control over the release date (perhaps between maximum and minimum limits set by the court) by the treating agent is advisable; as is the ability to recall a patient from parole if it is not going well, and if possible before any offence has been committed.

## What are the present difficulties?

There are so many psychopaths and so few facilities that sometimes nothing is done for them; they are often too difficult to be handled as out-patients and nearly all psychiatric hospitals refuse them. For those that are effectively handled, perhaps in Grendon hospital-prison or in one of the special units, there is not sufficient after-care of the sort that they require. Long-term supportive accommodation geared to their dependency and immaturity is very hard to come by.

Legislation provides all the compulsory treatment that could reasonably be required, but there are one or two points that need review. It would be helpful if certain approved prisons could be designed for the reception and treatment of Section 60 cases (Mental Health Act, 1959) if they had committed offences of appropriate seriousness. This would permit the transfer of criminal patients from hospital to prison when necessary, i.e. the reverse of Section 72 of the Mental Health Act. If the fixed sentence of life imprisonment for murder were abolished, there would be no further need to stretch the meaning of 'abnormality of mind' and of 'substantially impaired' simply to avoid a life sentence, and if at the same time treatment were available within the prisons the concept of diminished responsibility would become redundant.

The philosophy of Part 5 of the Mental Health Act, 1969, is to arrange for the treatment of psychopaths in the hospitals of the Department of Health, yet the hospitals are very reluctant, and rightly so, for they do not in general have the facilities. This policy is doubly faulty in that it embarrasses the hospitals and undermines the morale of the prison staffs who are able and willing to tackle the task but are denied the facilities and support. The policy of transferring treatment cases to hospital, implies that what is left in the prisons needs no treatment which is demonstrably wrong. The policy also discourages the prison medical service from taking part in the treatment of psychopaths. There are less than 100 doctors in this service; they are responsible for the routine 'public health' functions of the institutions as well as much of the general practice work of sick parades; in addition there are 14,000 psychiatric reports to make each year, and courts to be attended; there cannot be much time left for treatment, though there are some part-time visiting psychotherapists and some units which specialize in treatment.

Again, the special hospitals are so full that it is difficult to obtain transfers from the prisons and very disturbed psychopaths, sometimes subject to psychotic episodes, have to be accommodated in prisons. At one point the prisons in desperation evolve a psychopathic unit of their own, then plans are made to open new regional special hospitals; to the outsider there seems to be little co-ordination.

There is far too little community participation in the handling of psychopaths. Various schemes for voluntary associates have been tried but it is difficult to match the right offender with the right associate, and to prevent the relationships getting out of hand. Probably the best area in which to use the voluntary associate is in the after-care hostels, supporting a professional warden.

## Idealistic solution

The prisons are burdened with excessive numbers, outdated buildings, and limited finance. In consequence many of them are squalid, uninspired, and unable to help the large proportion of handicapped people who rotate through them. To effect a reform comparable to that which has occurred in the mental hospitals, it would first and foremost be essential to eliminate, if that were possible, the retributive image of the prison, regarding them instead as protective institutions.

Continuing the idealistic approach, no one should be imprisoned unless he is a definite danger to the community, and conversely anyone (whatever his characteristics or state) should be imprisoned if declared a danger to society by a court. Treatment facilities within prisons should be so effective that the need to transfer cases when they happen to be sick as well as criminal, should not arise. In assessing dangerousness a prospective view should be taken; the actual offence only being considered as one factor in assessing whether or not there will be another in the future. Thus even a very serious offender who is mentally ill might go to a psychiatric hospital if the risk of future offences is nil, whereas an offender who is also mentally ill and very likely to repeat his offences would be better placed in the protective institution (prison), where he could expect equally good treatment. Without this therapeutic atmosphere the prisons will not change. This would mean that the special hospitals should be restored to the prison service, bringing with them their tolerance, nursing skills, and their long experience of treating and releasing psychopathic and other patients. The ease of transfer through the wide variety of prison establishments, including open prisons, would greatly speed the turnover in these hospitals. At the same time ordinary prison officers and hospital officers from the prisons could circulate through these hospitals as they do to some extent through Grendon, and thus learn a new outlook. Section 60 (hospital orders) under the Mental Health Act could be made equally well to a prison or hospital, perhaps in the first place, according to the predilection of the court. The struggle to find an outside hospital willing to take such a case (often an essentially open hospital from which the patient will soon remove himself) would be avoided (8).

This would mean that the prison medical service should be unified with the national service.

It would make the diminished responsibility provision of Section 2 of the Homicide Act, 1947, meaningless, and avoid a great deal of absurd medical evidence in the assize courts. A man would either be guilty or not guilty of murder and would go to a protective establishment on an indeterminate (not a life) sentence, if necessary with a restriction order made by the court, but his treatment would be entirely a matter for the prison service.

At the lower end of the dangerousness scale, a host of drunken and minor offenders who could not be regarded as a danger to society would never be sentenced to prison, but rather referred to reception centres where their needs would as far as possible be discovered and a plan made. Possibly refusal or inability to co-operate with such a plan, together with renewed offences, might ultimately constitute a danger to the community and thus qualify for a prison.

Are all offenders to be regarded as sick, handicapped, and suitable material for social workers and doctors? Not at all: 70 per cent of first sentenced men are said not to return. This almost certainly means that they need never have served a sentence. Nearly all magistrates believe that the remand in custody is a useful treatment measure (though it may not legally be used as such). Psychologically a man will be at an optimum as regards capacity to change his outlook whilst on remand in custody. Thus remand in custody with a deferred sentence if properly used could empty our prisons of most of the short-term first offenders. I think magistrates should be allowed to use remands as treatment provided that an offence punishable with imprisonment has been proved. It is wrong that a magistrate cannot say to a man who has just been found guilty of an offence, and who has not co-operated with previous non-custodial methods, 'go back to the remand prison and think about it, and let me know why I should not now pass a sentence of imprisonment'.

It is perhaps too much to expect an indeterminate sentence except for extremely severe offences, and as an alternative the policy of making a sentence within stated limits, the upper being very substantial, is probably best, provided that the prisons are organized therapeutically and can be sufficiently flexible to operate a good parole system at an early date.

Finally it should be possible for anyone who has been an offender in the past and who is known to the protective service, to apply voluntarily for readmission. Without doubt if a genuinely helpful regime had been established, such voluntary re-admissions, probably for quite short periods, would be widely used and very useful. To anticipate very real concern about men who might be only too willing to give up and let the state support them, there would be properly organized industries within the service by which a man could be expected to contribute to his maintenance. In practice the wish for freedom is so strong that only the genuinely sick and profoundly psychopathic do not eventually want to be independent.

## The immediate task

If the term psychopath is to persist (and I am afraid it is now so built into our laws and literature that it will) we must learn to broaden the concept and to include in our thinking psychopaths wherever they appear, whether in Borstals and prisons, or hospitals, or reception centres and lodging-houses, because they drift about between these centres, which urgently need to be brought into closer relationship with one another.

One of the principal factors preventing such a relationship is the failure at nearly all levels to understand the place of punishment. First, it only works in those whose learning capacities are intact, and almost by definition the psychopath is thus immune to punishment. Second, it has an appalling history of failure with all the most troublesome offenders. Third, it is immensely expensive and exhausting to apply where custody is involved. If any progress is to be made with the penal system the penal-retributive motive must be dropped and the system looked upon as protective and therapeutic. Until the retributive element goes we shall not be able to bring the prisons into effective relationship with other community services.

### REFERENCES

1. CLECKLEY, H. (1955). *The Mask of Sanity* (St Louis: Mosby Co.).
2. MORRIS, P. (1969). *Put Away* (London: Routledge and Kegan Paul).
3. LEWIS, SIR A. (1953). 'Health as a social concept', *Br. J. Sociol.* **4**, 2.
4. SILBERMAN, M., and GIBBENS, T. C. N. (1966). *Royal London Prisoners' Aid Society Annual Report.*
5. GIBBENS, T. C. N. (1963). *Psychiatric Studies of Borstal Lads* (London: Oxford University Press).
6. SCOTT, P. D. (1964). 'Approved school success rates', *Br. J. Criminol.* **4**, 6, 525.
7. WEST, D. J. (1963). *The Habitual Prisoner* (London: Macmillan & Co.).
8. ROLLIN, H. R. (1969). *The Mentally Abnormal Offender and the Law* (Oxford: Pergamon Press).

# DISCUSSION

*People inside prison have been declared by the law to be guilty of an offence against society. Society outside prison is guilty of not providing adequate care and accommodation for those of its members who are inside. Few people would accept that it is yet possible to abolish prisons; few would disagree that prisons should be changed. One way to do this would be to reduce their population drastically by a more selective committal policy. Even with their antiquated, and often insanitary, buildings and their shortage of staff, they would then have a better chance of tackling effectively their job of protection and, more doubtfully, deterrence. Nor is this an unrealistic project. To protect society, prison care is probably only really necessary for the aggressive psychopath and the antisocial who has decided to make a living by crime. Its value as a deterrent is hotly debated. It may influence the calculations of the 'professional' criminal and his potential colleagues, but it probably has little effect on the psychopath in his moment of violence. Yet because some of the graver offences of the psychopath arouse a deep-seated need to exact retribution, the public is uneasy when what they consider to be too light sentences are imposed for such emotive crimes as baby-battering*

*Psychopaths form a large and intractable part of the prison population. (A satisfactory definition of this term has never been established, but it has now achieved legal status.) Apart from the small aggressive group, they are mostly inadequate people who, though they have a high nuisance value, are not a real danger to the community. When they are sent to prison their sentence is often accompanied by a hopeful reference to the psychiatric treatment they will receive there. In fact, too often, society is unloading one more insoluble problem on an already overburdened prison medical service. The only useful, and still tentative, method of treating these people is by a total regime of which the doctor is only a small part, and this therapy the doctor is, of course, unable even to attempt in prison surroundings. Resentment at being asked to do the impossible and to accept other people's failures is lowering the morale of the prison medical service.*

*Doubt about the effectiveness of psychiatric methods of treating prisoners is reinforced by the long-term results of the experimental hospital prison at Grendon, for short-term success with recidivists apparently falters after some two years. But this may be yet another proof of the need for more and better after-care and support rather than an indictment of progressive methods. One helpful innovation which is being introduced, partly at the instigation of the parole system, is the relaxation of the tradition that a man's crime is never mentioned once he is serving his sentence. This probably started as a well-meant desire not to rake up the past. But the past is usually relevant to the future, and constructive discussion of old difficulties may help and safeguard a prisoner when he returns to the community.*

*As Dr Scott pointed out, differences between the populations of our prisons and of our mental hospitals are not great enough to justify the differences between these two kinds of institution. Society has no right to segregate handicapped people for its own protection unless in return it offers adequate care for* their *protection.*

# 12

# Quality of survival

P. B. BEESON
MD, FRCP
*Nuffield Professor of Clinical Medicine*
*University of Oxford*

# Quality of survival

THE title of our conference, 'Patient, Doctor, Society', should have included a fourth party, i.e. government. Perhaps to all of you who have been participating in a National Health Service for more than twenty years this hardly needed saying, but in view of my background in another system of medicine the participation of government is the prominent characteristic of medical practice in this country.

I should like to look back on the broadly varied group of important problems we have considered in the last day-and-a-half and give you the perspective and priorities of one participant, especially with reference to the roles of the four parties in these different types of problem.

In the first group I would put the question of genetic pollution and of spina bifida. It was reassuring to hear the genetic experts, Dr Carter and Professor Harry Harris, say that they thought we had plenty of time to consider this threat and that in some of the possible problems about twenty-five generations would be required to bring about a serious new medical dilemma. The other question which I think belongs in this category, spina bifida and the baby with other severe congenital malformation, seems to me to be comparatively small in scope and manageable as contrasted with some of the other subjects. In general I think both of these can be left to medical science and the clinical practitioner. I think we should encourage genetics research and even genetic engineering. Regarding the latter, the recent success of Henry Harris and his collaborators at Oxford using the technique of cell fusion to incorporate a missing enzyme without at the same time conferring a new antigenic quality, while still an *in-vitro* phenomenon suggests a very possible way of approaching certain hereditary disorders in which an enzyme is lacking. The decision whether to try to salvage and repair a severely malformed infant probably must be made immediately by the obstetrician and his specialist *confrères*, largely without forcing such a decision on the parents. There is, as I see it, little scope in either of these problems for policymaking by government or society.

In the next category I would place all the expensive new life support systems that have come into fairly general use within the last decade; intensive care units, coronary care units, respiratory units, haemodialysis, and organ transplant. These are costly not only in terms of money but also in their secondary effects on the whole hospital in which they are organized. They strain the nursing resources and the laboratory resources. They are furthermore wholetime occupations of the physicians and surgeons who operate them. Of course they are desired by the doctors in an institution and aside from the fact that they save lives and make possible a tolerable existence for a few patients they have value as research tools and for the teaching of clinical medicine. Nevertheless, they are so costly, in the terms defined above, that we must recognize that to have these means to give up some other health activity or to render it less effective. It must be determined soon (1) how valuable these treatments are in terms of actual life-saving as well as of the quality of survival and (2) what other things could be done with the money and the skilled time that goes into the operation of such units. Although Dr Spencer has stressed the difficulties in making value judgements on such things as intensive care units I believe they can be evaluated by more or less the same techniques that the Medical Research Council has developed for combined clinical studies, and I think that the practising doctors would accept with good will a delay in policy to establish such units if it were understood that intensive and qualified study is under way.

With the advantage of hindsight it would be possible to argue now that the decision taken three or four years ago to establish chronic haemodialysis centres in all regions of the UK had not been the right decision. We have heard from Professor Calne that a major bottleneck is the supply of donor kidneys and one of the results is that increasing numbers of patients are now being held on chronic haemodialysis for indefinite periods of time. In Oxford alone the number of such people increases by about twenty per year. At present the haemodialysis unit of six beds must be supported by a like number of beds so that patients on home dialysis can be admitted periodically for the various problems that crop up in anyone on long-term dialysis therapy.

What lessons can we learn from this experience? First of all, the advisory committee which recommended a nationwide establishment was preponderantly composed of specialists in renal disease. Secondly, society and its representatives in Parliament created an almost irresistible pressure for this service as a result of articles about individual patients and their families in the press as well as radio and television discussion. So, if it were agreed that this had not been the best of all possible decisions then all four bodies concerned might have to share any blame attached.

I come now to a group of problems which dwarf all the preceding ones. The major one of these is the care of the aged, but in the same general category I would place the care of the mentally defective, the mentally ill, the severely crippled, and the psychotic prisoner. It seemed notable to me that Professor Anderson in discussing the geriatric problem did not say much about medical care. He chose to emphasize instead such things as post-retirement activities and housing. These subjects do indeed deserve to be considered under the topic of the *quality of survival*. There is, of course, an additional role for the doctor in all these groups of patients, but here the making of policy must be done by society acting through its elected representatives in government.

Now there is another aspect of the quality of survival which we have not touched on in this symposium, but which I think I was expected to deal with and that has to do with the troubling questions of prolonging life unnecessarily, with special emphasis on the increased technology available to maintain the function of the circulation and respiration, even when the brain is grossly damaged or when there is an irreparable disease process elsewhere. Here we must consider such things as the use of antibiotics to control what would otherwise be a fatal infection, the maintenance of fluid and electrolyte balance by parenteral injections, the undertaking of massive and deforming surgery in elderly patients to cure cancer, the use of cytotoxic drugs on the slim chance of ameliorating a neoplastic disease, etc. It is appropriate that such a topic be assigned to a general physician since we are the ones who deal with 'natural causes of death'. Indeed in the busy general medical service the expected death-rate is from 6 to 10 per cent of all patients admitted, so it can be assumed that we general physicians are always coping with problems of this nature.

No two people hold quite identical views but I can give you a few general statements to show how I feel.

(1) I would very much dislike to see the development of any legal policy of euthanasia. Doctors would have to be involved in such decisions and no matter what the safeguards we would lose a certain very important ingredient of medical care, namely, the conviction on the part of our patients that our main object is to help them. Once we became identified as possible executioners irreparable harm would have been done to doctor/patient relationships.

(2) The prolongation of life beyond the natural course of the disease concerned by use of modern techniques is not a common or frequent problem in medicine. Exceptional cases where comatose patients have been enabled to survive for long periods of time by the use of parenteral nutrition, etc., are so rare that they are likely to be reported in the newspapers and this has perhaps given rise to a belief that such instances are commonplace. In the vast majority of instances the natural course of disease is the mechanism of death.

(3) Although I have rejected euthanasia I have on the other hand no misgivings about the withholding of antibiotics and parenteral fluids in certain instances where beyond reasonable doubt the patient is hopelessly ill.

(4) Death deserves dignity. When the situation is irretrievable we should remove tubes from body orifices and needles from blood vessels. Routine measures to start the heart beating again after it has stopped naturally should not be permitted in such instances. (I must not be misinterpreted here as saying that cardiac arrest due to arrhythmia should not be vigorously treated.)

(5) For my own guidance I have found Trudeau's dictum ('. . . to comfort, always') immensely helpful. And comfort does not apply solely to the patient. The family must also be included. Most often comfort means compassion and 'staying with' the patient. Our most common sin is to desert dying people and find excuses for not coming in to see them. Comfort also means thoughtful use of

analgesia and symptomatic measures to control nausea, thirst, etc. Sometimes comfort means the use of aggressive methods of treatment and this applies particularly to patients with neoplastic disease. They and their families sometimes welcome the suggestion of high-risk surgery or the employment of drugs which are certain to have unpleasant side-effects.

(6) The expressed wishes of family and patient must be respected and generally agreed to. On the other hand, in a question of the type of decision which falls in the category of '. . . need'st not strive officiously to keep alive' the doctor should usually act on his own judgement. One cannot expect the family to have the experience or objectivity to make this decision and furthermore if they are in agreement at the time they may later suffer remorse.

(7) I think problems of the type I have been discussing represent one of the aspects of medical care in which an older doctor may excel.

So in conclusion it seems to me that policies relating to the general topic of quality of survival must be determined by different parties. I would leave the geneticists unfettered to learn all that they can about heredity. There are situations in which the doctor alone must determine policy based on the intimate nature of his relation with the patient, his family, and his life situation. There are others in which society acting through its representative government must make the decision. Increasingly ideal care becomes more and more expensive. It is going to be the task of government to decide on priorities in just the same way that it decides how many war planes, how many schools, or how many airports a country should have. We doctors will have to advise on some of these matters and if we are to give the best advice we must make our value judgements objectively, subordinating to the best of our ability our own special interests.

# DISCUSSION

*Much of life is dull, so the dramatic can always claim attention, the complex exciting techniques of medical advances are no exception. The treatment of spinal bifida, intensive care, dialysis, and transplant surgery have aroused public concern and secured a large share of public resources. But in fact the aggressive maintenance of life and the problems it brings is a small area of medical care compared with the less spectacular responsibilities which biological manipulation has created. Chief of these is the long-term care of the enormous and growing numbers of the handicapped and the old, yet these largely neglected people depend on the community for the quality of their survival during the extra years that have been thrust upon them.*

*Priorities in the allocation of medical resources are settled by the administrators in consultation with the medical profession. Too often these medical representatives have been enthusiastic experts in the new techniques, and the balance between large real needs and small esoteric needs has been lost. The mental health services and general practice have had too little opportunity to put forward the claims of the silent majority who are their patients. But now we seem to be coming to the end of unbridled technology. Unhappy, but dramatic, incidents have disclosed the neglected needs of the mental hospitals and, even more, of the mental deficiency institutions. Substantial material help is at last being given to them, and a determined effort has been launched to draw them back into the main stream of medicine. The GP is also being offered fresh opportunities. He is no longer isolated, and the growth of health centres and group practice now allows this specialty to take a more effective part in the organization of the profession. The GP is also strategically placed to share the research on health care and on the evaluation of treatment which must be tackled if the quality of survival is to be enhanced. The health centre can become the laboratory of the community, and it is already the joint workshop of many of the social disciplines which must share in these projects.*

*But no research is needed to recognize the plight of the handicapped and the old as our biggest social problem. Many of their needs differ, but one they have in common—the need for some satisfying occupation. To some extent we have created, or at least increased, the number of the handicapped. But the problem of old age is as old as man, and some other civilizations have dealt with it more successfully than ours. We seem to be prepared to accept too readily old age as an eventless interregnum before death, which itself is to be feared and postponed as long as possible. Yet death is as much a part of life as birth, and it would be more logical to fear the prolongation of life than death, were it not that our world too often deprives the process of dying of dignity. We must relearn the saying: 'Ce n'est pas un homme qui meurt; c'est un immortel qui commence.'*

# POSTSCRIPT

## BY SIR GEORGE PICKERING

A CENTURY ago the challenge to medicine was to save life. At that time a good deal was known about epidemiology and the effects of housing and sanitation on disease and death, though the light was just beginning to dawn on the mechanisms of disease. Where death could not be prevented, the patient's comfort was the prime object.

The relentless advance of science and technology has equipped man with new powers and new achievements and presented him with new problems, which he is only beginning to recognize, and with which he has yet to come to grips. Over-population, pollution, and the effects of atomic fission now stand out clearly as endangering man's indefinite existence on this planet, and no other, capable of sustaining his life, has been discovered. These three problems pose new and great unknowns for mankind. Given the will, they could be solved by the use of existing scientific knowledge by the end of the century. But alas, a sense of common purpose has not yet been aroused in mankind.

The issues which confront doctors today, in their professional lives, are of similar origin though more modest in scope. With modern antibiotics and modern machines it is possible to keep a semblance of life when the central nervous system has become unresponsive; without these machines the patient would indubitably be dead. The cost in terms of skilled manpower and other scarce resources is great. To what extent is it right to demand these from society? Organs can be taken after death and transplanted into those who are well but for the total failure of a vital organ. Demand exceeds supply and probably always will do. Here again society is faced with a moral and ethical dilemma.

Not only are there too many people in the world, but also too many are too old. As Dr Anderson has said, nowadays elderly women are almost immortal. Should an organ fail, a new one can be obtained. The exception is the brain. So the future holds out the possibility of an ageing population stuffed with other people's viscera and with their own senile brains.

These problems now facing society have been created by doctors and by medical science. They concern doctors but they also concern society at large. Indeed, the decisions that have to be made are those for society and for governments. Doctors can only inform and advise.

While many of the problems now facing society are to be laid at the door of success, there are some which represent the failure of medical science. Some are probably insoluble, except by birth control on eugenic lines, like spina bifida; when the infant is born the damage has already been done. But there is one outstanding problem which is probably soluble and which has not yet been solved. This is the problem of mental disease. In every highly developed country this represents the sector of disease consuming the largest *tranche* of money and of medical, nursing, and social care. The increasingly strident voice of social scientists, politicians, and administrators, might say here is a splendid example of failure in the planning and direction of scientific research. The facts show how ignorant they are of what they are talking about and the utter sterility and irrelevance of the application of cost-benefit analysis to scientific research. For the magnitude and social importance of the problem has been evident for half a century to every major agency supporting medical research, whether financed from public funds or private charity. They have accordingly made it known that they are increasingly willing to support projects in this field and have gone out of their way to establish research units. And yet nothing much has happened. The cost has been huge, the benefits slight—a cost-benefit analysis would show indeed the financial irresponsibility of those charged with supporting medical research. As one of those who has been responsible, I have become painfully aware that it is an unprofitable exercise to organize a large and expensive hunt, unless one knows for what one is hunting. The master facts still escape us, and they will be discovered, as they always have been, by chance, and the prepared mind. The point is illustrated by the one mental disease whose mechanism is reasonably well understood, phenylketonuria. Folling was testing the urine of mentally defective children with ferric chloride, a reagent used to detect diabetes, when he noticed one turn green. He followed this up and showed that a very few mentally defective children suffer from a simple inherited enzymatic defect in which the metabolism of the amino-acid, phenylalanine, is arrested at the stage of phenyl ketone which accumulates in the tissues preventing mental development. No Secretary of the Medical Research Council, no Chairman of Trustees of the Rockefeller Foundation, and no President of the United States could have ordered the discovery of the nature of this disease because no one knew where to look.

These simple facts about medical research are extremely galling to those who 'direct' it, since their impotence is thus displayed, but most encouraging to those who prosecute it, since there is still an opportunity, open to all, to win undying fame. Despite the gloomy outlook of Sir Macfarlane Burnet, there is still a future, and still an adventure to be found, in medical research.

This volume now draws to its close. Its function has been to display problems that can be solved only by doctors, patients, and society acting in concert. This has not always happened in the past, partly due to human frailty and partly because of faulty presentation. To make a small contribution to the latter has been the objective of those who organized and conducted the meeting here reported.